This book is dedicated to the memory of
Gobgaew Najpinij 1941 to 2016
known to her students as
"Mae" (Mother)

Recipes by Mae - written by her
most grateful students
Carole Mason and Ning Najpinij

Contents

About Mae

Kobkaew (pronounced Gobgaew), who I was honoured to call Mae (meaning mother), was born in Udon Thani in 1941 into a large family of eight children. They lived in a stilted wooden house where sophisticated food was not overly important to her family who concentrated all their efforts on making their living as agricultural traders and sugar producers and processors. Her mother was quite a well known local character who rode around the village on a horse.

They cooked simply and ate traditional food, basing their meals around the usual rice, nahm prik and fried fish dishes that were common to the period and region.

However even as a child Mae was fascinated with the heritage of Thai food and yearned to understand and learn more about it.

Her chance came in her late teens when she went to stay with an aunt who ran a refined household and who aided her passion for ancient Thai food. She taught her to cook in the Royal manner and passed on much of her knowledge.

During this time Mae also had a talented teacher called Somsir who was skilled in many ancient Thai handicrafts, she helped Mae to master many intricate skills which later helped her with fruit carving and presentation.

Motivated by the progress she had made, Mae moved to Bangkok to attend the prestigious Suan Dusit finishing school for young ladies. A world away from Udon Thani, this school was very strict, and to succeed there, Mae was driven to hone her skills to perfection in presentation and flavour balancing. Throughout her life she upheld the same standards that were instilled within her there.

After completing her Higher Certificate in Home Economics she went on to complete a BA in food and nutrition at Prasanmitr University.

In her twenties she married and had two children, Ning and a son who is a Buddhist monk in a forest hermitage in Thailand.

She then began a teaching career, retiring as Assistant Professor at Suan Dusit University in Bangkok and during this time she wrote two books which are still used in teaching establishments today.

After she retired she was in great demand throughout the world giving consultancy and training to many famous restaurants such as Thai Amarin in Washington, Cool Basil in California and Banjarong in India.

She was featured in articles in Tatler, Vogue USA, Portuguese news and Australian Gourmet Magazine.

She appeared on several TV programmes including a US documentary and several cooking and chatting TV and radio programmes in Thailand.

In 1995 she made a Thai dessert for the World Leader Chefs conference (chefs from Royal families all over the world gather to exchange ideas and recipes) where she had the great honour to present her work to Crown Princess Mahachakri Sirindhorn. She subsequently devised and developed some recipes for Thai Airlines as part of a marketing campaign.

She appeared as a guest lecturer at the three most prestigious universities in Bangkok, Thammasat, Mahidol and Chulalongkorn and taught students from China, Japan, Bali, UK, USA, Spain, Italy and Switzerland.

Mae lent her support to many published authors such as Chef Robert Danhi and Chai Siriyan, and her recipes appear in David Thompson's books, "Thai Food" and "Thai Street Food".

RECIPES
with kind permission of Kobkaew Najpinij
WRITER
Carole Mason
CONSULTANT
Ning Najpinij
DESIGNER
Michelle Bastock
PHOTOGRAPHY
Carole Mason
Historical photos used with the kind permission of Kobkaew Najpinij

A CIP record of this book is available at The British Library.

First edition printed in the UK in 2017
by Think Digital Books
ISBN 978-1-9999270-0-4
This book can also be ordered from
Carole Mason on www.corianderroute.co.uk

NOTES:

Recipes in this book are designed to serve two unless otherwise stated.

This is so that you can select more than one dish to serve at a meal. Try and choose something salty, something sour, something sweet and something bitter in each meal. Also make sure that you use several cooking styles in each meal, a combination of steamed, grilled and curried for instance.

All spoon measurements are level and all eggs are medium.

About Carole and Ning

I was in my early 20"s by the time I made my first visit to Thailand and it was love at first sight!
Whilst my holiday friend discovered the joys of scuba diving I indulged in learning about Thai food and quickly found places to learn, in a plethora of kitchens, restaurants and street stalls.
I was constantly looking over somebody's shoulder trying to unravel the mysteries of this wonderful cuisine I had just discovered.

From then onwards I returned to Thailand whenever possible and did everything I could to learn more. I went on simple tourist courses, extravagant cooking holidays, wheedled my way into the kitchens of restaurants and made friends with many keen home cooks. When I came home I would devour any new cookbooks, research Thai ingredients and scour the country for them. My passion for Thailand grew so much I even got married there.

In 2005 my lucky break came .... I met Mae whilst I was on a course in Thailand, just after she retired, we became friends and started to cook together. I still worked full time in the UK but I would sometimes visit for four month stretches and we would work together in the kitchen. I think we must have spent a year together in a kitchen in total! It was wonderful and I miss those days so much.

During the last few years I have become aware that it is very difficult to buy coriander root in the UK, especially outside of London, and I have set up a website to try and attract the attention of a major supermarket to encourage them to stock the root and improve supply for us all.
I have also been running supper clubs in my home cooking Mae's recipes.

I have written this book with Ning's help to showcase my favourite recipes as taught to me by Mae as a tribute to her and I hope that you love them like I do.

Carole Mason X
www.corianderroute.co.uk

Ning Najpinij is Mae's daughter. She has spent her life cooking at her mothers side and was inspired to take up food as a career.

Since studying in both Thailand and the USA she has amassed extensive hospitality experience and she has worked at Suan Dusit University Culinary School as a lecturer since 1988.
Ning also has a PhD in Thai Studies on the subject of Thai Gastronomy from Chulalongkorn University.

She is a co-founder of the innovative Bangkok Bold Cooking Studio where in addition to teaching she offers advice on food culture and trends, food styling and lecturing.

She has undertaken extensive consultancy work including the organising of a Thai food tour and assisting with a TV program for widely acclaimed chef, author and food historian David Thompson.
She has provided consultancy for many International restaurants and assists with product development for major food producers such as Dole. She has been a visiting lecturer for all the major Universities in Bangkok and is a familiar face on the podium at the Culinary Institute of America.

Why we love coriander root!

Coriander root is the heart and soul of Thai cooking. It is the foundation upon which many dishes are built. It not only adds taste, texture and depth but it enables the user to create the foundation pastes that give Thai food its unique flavour.
Sadly this unique flavour is very quickly being lost.
Both in the UK and indeed in Thailand the use of pre-made pastes is becoming widespread. Although there are some good pre-made curry pastes out there, curry is only scratching the surface of the role of coriander root and I hope that this book will encourage you to join my campaign for the root and discover the joys of this beleaguered ingredient.

Currently it is not easy to get your hands on coriander root in the UK, the coriander which is abundant today is often sold with the root cut off.
I despair of this but it is simply due to the lack of understanding of its value.

Coriander root is as fundamental to Thai food as the onion is to British food.

Just imagine the limits to your cooking without this British staple!
One of the things that really worries me is that without the root Thai people who come to live in the UK are not able to pass on their food heritage to their children.
Without coriander root many dishes are severely compromised and the understanding of its use in the food culture is lost.
There are many dishes based around what I call "magic paste". That is coriander root pounded in a pestle and mortar with some coarse salt, whole white peppercorns and garlic. These four essentials are the foundation of many a magical dish.
The range of Thai food you can cook without this paste is severely restricted.

But how do we get the root?

Hmm - this is a problem that has haunted me for many sleepless nights, and why I started my blog www.corianderroute.co.uk to draw attention to the importance of this key ingredient and hopefully persuade one of the major supermarkets to supply and stock the root and make this fantastic food heritage available for all.

If there is a demand then a supply will follow - it's a simple business principle.

Maybe if enough of us ask loudly enough then a supermarket may well hear our plea.

Carole Mason x

Coriander trader in the night flower market

Carole's Thai pantry essentials and getting prepared...

Real coconut milk is the best!

When I go to Thailand I am always envious of their lovely, silky smooth, rich and delicious coconut milk. In the early morning, in every market, coconuts are being processed in giant shredding machines and industrial presses, making coconut milk and cream that is ideal for cooking.

In the UK however it's a different story, even the coconuts we get are inferior, and so it is quite difficult to get the consistency and taste that I want.
When I am back in Blighty it is an ingredient that I am forced to reluctantly compromise on and I would like to share with you how I do this.

I crack coconuts by hitting them hard with the blunt side of a cleaver then turning them - repeat this as many times as necessary and you will find that the coconut will crack neatly down the middle.
Allow the thin liquid to run away down the sink (you don't need it) or catch it in a bowl, sieve it and drink it or use it to steam mussels.
Remove all the coconut meat with an oyster shucker and put it into a strong blender.
Cover with hot but not boiling water and blend until smooth.

Put a muslin cloth in a strainer or over a glass jug and pour the blended coconut milk in small batches then squeeze out the juice and discard the pulp.
Finally you will have coconut milk and cream in one. If you leave this to settle for about fifteen minutes then the coconut cream will float to the top. You can now skim the cream off and you are ready to make the perfect curry.

That is the best technique I have found but it is seldom ideal as the coconut cream is not thick enough to use for everything. It is for this reason that throughout the book, where it aids the dish to have very thick coconut cream, I have suggested that you use canned.

I wouldn't however use canned coconut milk to make a curry as this just makes the final dish too cloying.

Another tip that may help you, which I sometimes use in desperation, is to mix powdered coconut milk with real coconut milk to boost the flavour without it becoming too gloopy or artificial.

To give you an idea of how many coconuts to buy for the recipes you need a kilo of coconut meat to make 750ml of combined coconut milk and cream which is about three cups.

Make sure the coconuts are heavy with liquid when you buy them by shaking them.

Making real milk may sound like hard work but you can do it beforehand and store it in the fridge and the difference it makes to the end result is phenomenal.

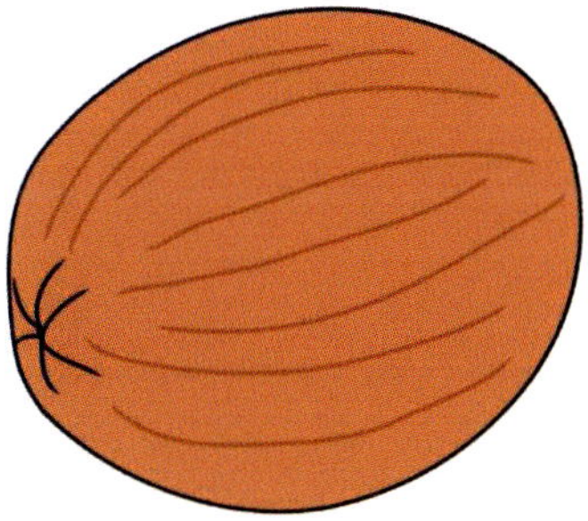

Coconut

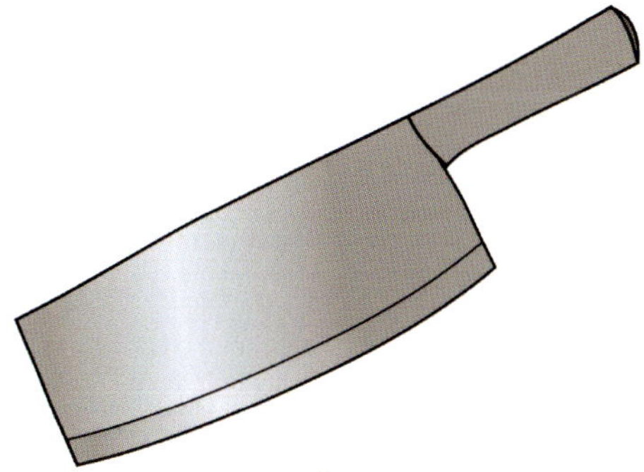

CRACK

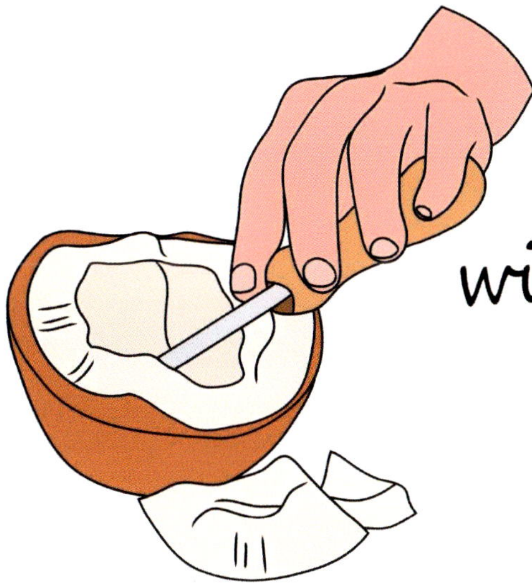

Remove the meat with an oyster shucker

BLEND

Strain Through Muslin

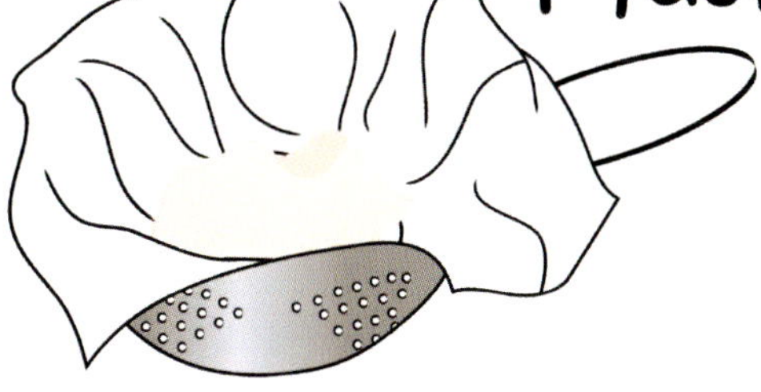

Allow to split into milk and cream

Chopping and meat preparation...

An invaluable tool in my Thai kitchen is a big Chinese cleaver. I use the blunt side to crack open coconuts and it's essential for chopping meat on the bone and mincing meat. In this book I often ask for the meat to be chopped by hand with a cleaver. To do this run the blade through a garlic clove then chop by hitting repeatedly, flipping the meat over and repeating.

The best cleavers are the ones with an integrated metal handle because they go in the dishwasher and never break.

Season your wok...

A seasoned wok is a marvellous thing - when you first buy it, wash it with soapy warm water, rinse and let it dry naturally. Coat the inside lightly with vegetable oil by rubbing it on with paper kitchen towel and bake it in a hot oven for an hour at its highest setting. Take it out and allow it to cool then wash again with soap and really hot water. Repeat this process two or three times until a black coating covers the surface. Alternatively you could buy a non stick version.

A little BBQ...

Quite a few recipes in this book ask for you to BBQ some ingredients, usually to put in a paste, and although you could do these on the flame of the cooker you lose an authentic smoky back taste to the food so I think its worth the effort. The best way of dealing with this is just to have a small BBQ as it saves on both fuel and time. Sometimes I use the disposable ones which are effortless.

Stock making...

Home-made stocks are essential to cooking Thai food especially as many recipes are so finely balanced that a stock cube would just overwhelm their taste and ruin them.

If you really don't have time to make stock then use water instead rather than resorting to anything commercially made - however organic it sounds!

You can freeze stock and quickly defrost it or you can make it on the spot.

To make **chicken stock** use a couple of chicken wings or thighs on the bone. Cover them with water then add another 3 inches of water, half a dozen white peppercorns, 2 garlic cloves, half an onion peeled, a lump of peeled ginger, some coriander root and ideally Chinese celery but if you don't have that use any veg lying around. Bring to the boil and simmer for thirty minutes then strain, discard the solids and use or freeze the stock. When using frozen stock put a knob of ginger in when you reheat it - it just freshens it up.

For **vegetable stock** do the same but omit the chicken and simmer for one hour.

To make a light **fish stock** use water, any fish or bones, ginger, salt and a leafy green veg. Simmer for 15 minutes only as you do not want the stock to overwhelm the taste of the dish you are cooking.

Steaming...

Where a recipe calls for steaming, any steaming equipment you currently have will be fine. I have a wok with a steamer on top and that is ideal because it is broad with a glass lid and you can really see what's going on. However sometimes I opt for the bamboo Chinese steamers and line them with leafy vegetables especially if I am going to serve in them. An electric steamer is ok too.

Rice cooking...

Steamed jasmine rice

I'm a big fan of the electric rice cooker - simply measure the rice out, add water and within twenty minutes it's cooked! Best of all it keeps warm for up to five hours. It's one less thing to worry about.

Sticky rice (aka glutinous rice)

Although you can use a rice cooker for sticky rice I always go the traditional route because I find the end result so much more pleasing. With this system you use a traditional hourglass shaped steamer and a bamboo cone. The cone is lined with a muslin cloth and the rice is steamed inside it. You can buy an aluminium steamer and bamboo cone in most oriental shops for this.

Dry fried ground rice

This is often used as a salad or dip topping to add texture and crunch. To make this, dry fry sticky rice until it is golden and smells cooked. Allow it to cool then grind to a medium powder. You don't want the pieces too big or you will break your teeth!

Pestle and mortars and making pastes...

In my humble opinion there are many possible ways to modernise the cooking of Thai food but paste making is not one of them so let me explain why...

Although the cooking world has moved on with the vast array of food processors, blenders and grinders on offer, in actual fact the only way to fully release and blend the aromatic spices and herbs that make a classic Thai paste is in the traditional way by hand with a pestle and mortar.

If you use a mechanical blade to do the job the ingredients are torn and the resultant paste just does not come together in the same way. Quite simply the result will not be as good.

Therefore my absolute staple in the kitchen is a big stone pestle and mortar. I have several types actually but the stone one is crucial and everything I cook revolves around it. You need a good solid stone version, the ceramic versions often found in European kitchens will not hold up to the pounding and although the wooden pestle and mortars are great for making som tam salad the traditional stone sets are essential to paste making. Seek out one that holds around two cupfuls of ingredients minimum. They are quite easy to get hold of in the UK, see the listing at the end of this section for a supplier list.

The good news is that these pastes will last for about a week, in a sealed glass jar in the fridge, and they are not difficult to make. It just takes time and practice.

The best way to work is to hold the pestle at the top loosely and pound using a firm but light action.
Make sure that your wrist is loose otherwise it will make your muscles really sore and you won't be able to pound for very long.

Always use the pestle and mortar on a mat to reduce the impact both on yourself and the surface.
Clean the pestle and mortar with warm soapy water but if it starts to smell soak it for an hour with some diluted white rice vinegar then rinse it out.

Thai pastes use pretty much the same ingredients as one another so once you have been shopping it makes sense to make up a batch of several pastes at a time for later use.

Paste-making technique...

To make a paste - first prepare all the ingredients.

Chop the dried chillies into 5cm pieces and soak them until they are soft then split them open and remove all the seeds. Pound in a pestle and mortar with a pinch of coarse sea salt until you have a smooth paste.

Now add each ingredient one by one - the hardest ones first - but grind each one fully into the paste before moving onto the next. This is a really important tip so don't be tempted to rush.
Finally add the dried spices and shrimp paste. Pound them in and then give them a final stir.

Gobgaew presenting her Thai dessert for the "World Leader Chefs" event at Vimanmek Mansion in 1995 where the personal chefs of many world leaders came to share their knowledge.

That's Magic Paste!

The Joy of Magic Paste

There are many dishes based around what I call "Magic Paste". This paste is simply whole white peppercorns pounded in a pestle and mortar until finely ground, then coriander root, coarse sea salt and garlic are added and pounded until a paste is created. These four essentials are the foundation of many a magical dish.

The range of Thai food you can cook without coriander root is severely restricted. Many people will say that if you cannot get it you can use the leaves as a substitute but in my experience you cannot do this successfully.

Thai root is so strongly flavoured and, importantly, very dry. Therefore when you make a paste it holds its structure well and you can achieve a balance of coriander and garlic flavours without making the paste sloppy.

If you use leaves as a substitute the curry paste becomes too wet and you can never get the weak flavouring to balance with the garlic.

Also some say that you can use the roots from the supermarket herb pots but in my experience you have exactly the same problem with them.

If you seriously want to experience the full flavour of these dishes you need to get your hands on proper Thai root - it's nectar of the Gods!

Because root is so difficult to get in the UK I have tried to balance the recipes in the book. Many are for when you get the precious roots in your hands but I have also added plenty of recipes to use when you don't have any. In the index I have indicated dishes that use the root in pink.

N.B. The recipes without root are not compromised, they are authentic Mae recipes that never did use root.

When you finally get your hands on some roots you will need to clean them well. Depending how dirty they are, I either use a knife to scrape away the soil, or at worst, soak them in cold water. However, you must make sure you dry them thoroughly before storing away or they will rot.

The best thing to do is to immediately cut the roots from the leaves. You use both the leaves and roots in cooking but the leaves go off faster than the roots if you don't use them. The leaves can only be used fresh. Store the roots separately in the fridge in an airtight container for about a week.

If you put the roots in an airtight plastic box and put them in the freezer they will keep for several months.

Although they are never as good as when they are fresh I find them acceptable and it's certainly better than being rootless!

The spices used in this book are...

Bay Leaves: These are the usual bay leaves we get in the UK. It is best to use them fresh but you can keep a small plant outside all year round or alternatively keep some in the freezer.
Chinese Curry Powder: The Chinese type of curry powder is needed because it is fruitier and lighter than the Indian version.
Chillies: dried long red chillies are fundamental to paste making, look for some that are at least 3 inches long and still have some bend in them. They need to be kept in the dark, ideally in a fridge if you are keeping them for a long time as this keeps them in better condition. You should also get some smaller ones that are less than one inch.
You also need some **chilli powder** and **dried chilli flakes.** To make your own dried chilli flakes, dry fry some large dried chillies, allow to cook and then process in a coffee grinder.
See also fresh chillies in the herb section.
Cinnamon Sticks: These keep for longer in the dark.
Cloves: Readily available in Indian shops.
Coriander Seeds and Cumin Seeds: These seeds are almost always used dry fried in pastes so it is best to dry fry a batch, process them in a coffee grinder and store them in a jar for future use.
Fennel Seeds: Readily available in Indian shops.
Gaeng Hang Lae Powder: You can buy good commercial powder in oriental shops but if not this is my simple emergency recipe for it. I prefer to use the more complex gaeng hang lae powder but this works.
This recipe makes 3 tablespoons.
1 tablespoon of dry roast coriander seeds
2 1/2 teaspoons of cumin seeds
2 star anise dry fried and ground
1 inch piece of cassia bark dry fried and ground
2 white Thai cardamoms dry fried, seeds removed and ground
Mace: This is the outer sheath of the nutmeg. Buy it whole and store it. It keeps for a long time.
Makhwaen Pepper: This is a specialist northern Thai spice often called prickly ash. Sometimes you can find it in oriental shops but if not replace it with Szechuan pepper.
Ma Lhap: This is a northern Thai spice. If you can't get it replace it with fennel seeds.
Nutmeg: I tend to store this whole and powdered as both versions are useful.
Pepper: You should stock **black peppercorns** and I use so many **white peppercorns** that I keep some by the cooker in a little pot. You may occasionally need **long pepper** which can usually be found in Indian and Pakistani shops labelled pippali or peepar.
See also **young green peppercorns** in the herb section.
Proh Horm: This is is also known as aromatic or sand ginger and can often be bought in Chinese stores under the name Sha Jiang. It is actually dried galangal.
Star Anise: It is best to buy these whole and process a batch in a coffee grinder and then keep both forms on one side in a jar.
White Cardamom Pods: These are quite difficult to get but if you really can't find them replace them with **green cardamoms.**

Store-cupboard ingredients to have to hand...

Agar Agar: This is a gelatine setting agent. Although you can buy it in strips, I tend to use the powdered version. You need to boil it to get it to set but follow the manufacturers instructions. It does deteriorate, so when you use it, eat what you made on the same day.
Alum Rock Crystal: You will often find this in Indian shops, I use it to make sticky rice shine but in the past it was used to make bread whiter.
Bamboo Shoots: Because these are so difficult to get hold of in the UK I tend to use canned which are readily available.
Beancurd or Tofu: There is a vast range of product available, I tend to use the silken type as I find it easier to work with.
Dried Shrimp / Prawns: Look for ones that are the darkest colour and store them in the fridge.
Flour: Throughout the book I use **tapioca flour, arrowroot flour, cornflour, rice flour** and **glutinous rice flour**. In some recipes I tell you how to make tempura batter but you could also keep a ready mixed powder in stock if you like.
Noodles: kanom jeen noodles are made from rice flour and can be bought dried in the UK.
I also use **glass noodles** which can often be bought fresh or dried.
Nuts: The book calls for **cashew nuts** and **peanuts.** You need to find unsalted raw versions.
Sugar: palm sugar is a beautiful thing in Thailand but in the UK I can only find inferior solid bullet versions of it. I find it helps if you soften it in the microwave with a drop of water. I also call for **granulated white sugar** and **caster sugar** in this book but you can use caster sugar for all of these recipes. If you only have granulated sugar you can process that in a blender to make it finer.
Pickled Garlic: Is available in oriental stores in jars and keeps for a long time.
Pickled Mustard Greens: These can be bought in little bags in oriental stores but they have a chemical taste so soak and rinse them really well before use.
Pig Intestine: I use these for stuffing sausages and I much prefer them to the thick man-made casings. If you are lucky your local butcher will supply them or even stuff the sausages for you but if not you can buy them online, salted, and they last for quite a while in the fridge.
Rice Pancakes: are a great thing to keep in the pantry and they make it easy to put together a quick snack.
Salt: You will need **fine table salt** for some dishes and **coarse sea salt** for when you are making pastes.
Sesame Seeds: white sesame seeds are used in this book but you could replace with **black** ones.
Shrimp Paste: This is an essential element of Thai cooking and it keeps for a long time in the fridge.
Often there is a waxy covering on the shrimp paste when you buy it, just throw that away before the first use.
Always dry fry or heat in the microwave for a few seconds before using.
Split Mung Beans: These are often used in desserts, they are easy to find in Indian shops.
Tamarind Juice and Paste: I prefer to use the **blocks of tamarind**, soak it in hot water then strain. That is because I can control the taste and thickness of the paste myself. However there are many commercially prepared versions that are fine to use.
Nahm Prik Pow aka Chilli Jam: In this book I give you a recipe for a homemade version which is far superior and keeps in the fridge for months but I have listed it here in case you want to look for a commercial version.
Soybeans: I tend to use the whole **yellow** version in a jar and rinse them through before using.
Water Chestnuts: Readily available canned, if you have any spare put them in a plastic tub in the fridge in their own liquid.

Bottles, sauces and sundries to keep in stock...

Tienne Op Candle or Jasmine Essence: The traditional way to scent water or coconut with jasmine is to use a Tienne Op candle. I use a tin to do this so that the candle does not burn the container. The candles are difficult to get in the UK but, if you do you manage to buy one, store it in the fridge in a plastic container and it will last indefinitely. To scent water or coconut milk light the candle at both ends and allow it to burn for a few minutes.

Blow the candle out and quickly put it into the bottom of the tin next to the coconut milk, water or desserts and put the lid on. Place in the fridge for at least an hour. The smoke will gently infuse and impart a soft sandalwood-like essence. If you can't get the candle then simply use a commercially bought essence.

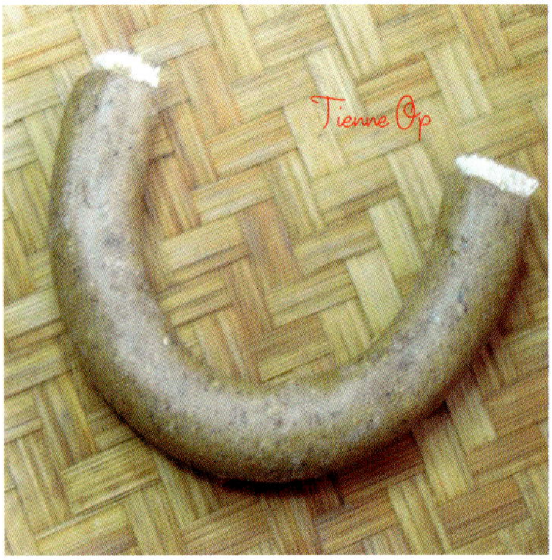

Fish Sauce: Try and buy a good version in the Asian supermarkets in a glass bottle as the small plastic bottles in the supermarkets can taste too artificial. In the bottom of the bottle you will see crystals that look like broken glass. Don't worry about these, they are normal. Once opened you can keep it for a few months and you don't have to put it in the fridge.

Hales Blue Boy: This comes in a variety of colours and I have used red in this book. It keeps for months once opened you don't have to refrigerate it.

Maggi Seasoning: This famous seasoning is used in oriental and other cuisines so is readily available.

Oyster Sauce: Buy this in a glass bottle and it will keep for months out of the fridge.

Sriracha Sauce: This is a great little sauce to have in the pantry, it keeps a long time and goes with almost everything.

Soy Sauce: In this book I mainly use **light soy sauce** but some recipes also use **black soy sauce** and **dark soy sauce.**

Vegetable Oil: I use this for both shallow and deep frying but you could also use sunflower oil.

Vinegar: I use a lot of **white rice vinegar** but **black vinegar** is in a couple of the recipes and also makes a great dip for deep fried food.

Fresh herbs I used in this book..

Basil: Thai basil: This herb dies so quickly and loses its flavour in the fridge. I usually just leave it in a cool place in winter but if you are not going to use it on the day of purchase store it upright in a bit of water inside a sealed plastic box in the fridge. It has an aniseed flavour and is essential to many curries and stir fry dishes.
I also often include it when serving a raw side salad. **Holy Basil:** This form of basil works really well in fish dishes.

Betel Leaves: These are used to make miang khem and the nearest replacement is firm spinach leaves.

Chives: In this book I have used chives to tie up some little parcels and you may find that our chives are not resilient enough for that. You could consider **Chinese chives** as an alternative, however they are stronger tasting. If not, cut some strips of pandanus leaves or banana leaf to do the job instead.

Chillies: Birds Eye Chillies: These tiny chillies also known as **scuds** are super hot and are really essential in making green curry paste. **Green Finger Chillies** are easy to find in Indian shops and again are used to make pastes. **Long Red chillies** are often used in strips as decoration, they are not as hot as some of the smaller versions. I also occasionally use **medium red** and **yellow chillies** for specific dishes.

Coriander Roots: To store them, chop off the green leaves and store the roots in an airtight plastic container. They will last in the fridge for about a week but you can put them in the freezer and use them straight from frozen. You can't defrost them and use them as they turn to mush.

Coriander Leaves: These are easy to get in supermarkets but the Indian shops sell bigger bunches much cheaper.

Sawtooth Coriander: This can usually only be found in Thai shops, it is similar to coriander but has a stronger taste and is lovely in salads.

Galangal, Grachai and Ginger: Galangal is similar to ginger but drier and more peppery. It keeps for a long time ideally in the fridge in a plastic bag. **Grachai** is wild ginger and comes as a cluster of pencil like shapes, it's peppery and fragrant and can also keep quite a while stored in the fridge in a plastic bag. **Ginger** is readily available and I generally keep it out of the fridge as it lasts a long time.

Garlic: Thai garlic is smaller and less pungent but you can use any garlic.

Kaffir Lime: Kaffir lime leaves are used a lot and they are usually available in oriental shops in the UK. Fresh is best but you can also freeze them and use them from frozen or defrost them. Do not buy the dried leaves they will not work. It is not possible for the **whole kaffir lime** fruit to be imported to the UK at the moment, so if you want to use these it is very frustrating. However you can buy and keep the plants and they are quite easy to keep and grow. The other alternative for paste making is to buy the dried version and reconstitute it before putting it in the paste. As a last resort If you really can't find these then just omit the zest needed from the recipe.

Lemongrass: This long stalky plant is a trademark of Thai cooking. If you can find the full long version buy this rather than the chopped-off supermarket version because it keeps so much longer. It should be rock solid when you buy it, not bendy. It will keep for a week in the fridge but if you have excess then very finely slice it and it will freeze. Never use the dried lemongrass as it lacks the oil so it just will not work.

Mint: When this book calls for mint any type will do.
Pandanus Leaf: These leaves are normally sold in packets in oriental shops. You can keep them in the fridge but they dry out in less than a week. One alternative is to buy a commercial essence for flavouring.
Tangerine juice: If you can't get tangerine use satsuma or clementine instead.
Turmeric: The important thing to know about fresh turmeric is that it is not interchangeable with dried turmeric which is different altogether. Also please be aware that, as with powdered turmeric, it stains both the hands and work surfaces so be careful.
Young Green Peppercorns: These are an essential ingredient in jungle curry but they do not keep well. They blacken within a few days in the fridge and do not freeze well so put them inside a plastic tub in the fridge and use them as soon as possible.

Fruit and vegetables I used in this book..

The vegetables marked with * are often eaten raw to accompany a dip or salad.

Acacia leaves: Fabulous in an omelette these leaves are often found in oriental shops.
*Aubergine aka Eggplant: Several types of aubergine are used in Thai cooking, the most distinctive type that everyone will recognise from green chicken curry are pea aubergines. These tiny eggplants come in clusters and are the size of peas. They are firm, dense and packed with seeds and when cooked they add texture to a dish. Long green aubergine are used to make a wonderful smokey BBQ salad but you can replace these with the more easily sourced red aubergine which we get in the UK.
*Apple Aubergines are the size of plums and come in a range of colours.
Banana: You can use any type of banana for the recipes in this book.
*Banana Blossom: This is a long dark burgundy vegetable about 6 inches long. When you remove the outer petals you will find a row of tiny bananas. You need to remove these to reveal the core. Put it into a bowl with water and sliced lemon and lemon juice then refrigerate until ready to use. It can be sliced and eaten raw or used as an ingredient in salad. You should wear gloves to do this otherwise your hands will be stained with a dark sap which you will have to remove with lemon juice.
Banana Leaves: Banana leaves can often be bought fresh or frozen in the UK but fresh is better as they tend to go brown when they are defrosted.
Bitter Melon: As its name indicates this can be very bitter. This can be reduced by salting it and washing in water but sometimes you really want it to be bitter so it is not a problem.
*Beans: Any type of beans can be used but generally Thai recipes call for wing beans or snake beans.
Bok Choy or Pak Choy: A leafy vegetable often used for stir fry.
*Cabbage: Cabbage is often eaten raw as an accompaniment and it is a great way to eat your greens.
The Thai chef usually rips rather than cuts vegetables but obviously this depends how leafy the greens are. If you have a firm cabbage like spring cabbage then you can either slice it or cut it into squares.
*Carrots: I usually cut these into batons for salads.
*Chinese Celery: Is leafier, stronger and more pungent than standard celery and it keeps well in the fridge.
*Cucumbers: You can use any kind of cucumber, the normal sized versions roll cut or cut into batons or the mini version for an extra touch of glamour.
Daikon: Is a cylindrical vegetable about 12 inches long but sometimes it is sold in pieces. Peeled and grated it is used to tenderise seafood and it can also be shaped into balls for deep frying or it can be finely sliced and added to soup. Look for daikon that is heavy and smooth, not wrinkled.

***Edible Flowers: Jasmine flowers** are great to use for Thai desserts but are difficult to source in the UK. If you can't get them just omit them or substitute with any edible flowers you can buy.
Gourd: Snake gourd is ideal to use for Thai cooking but any kind of gourd can act as a substitute.
***Lettuce:** Any version of lettuce is suitable to use but the crispy styles are best.
Kaffir Limes: See the notes in the herbs section.
Jackfruit: The large ripe jackfruit is suitable for desserts - the smaller hard ones are used in curry.
Logan: In season you can get these fresh but I find it satisfactory to use the canned version.
***Mango: Green mango** is unripe mango and it is used for salads and is added to soup. When shopping pick a firm one that is heavy with a dark green skin. **Sweet mango** Is super sweet and soft and is used for desserts. The loveliest ones are often found in the Indian stores in the UK.
Morning Glory: A versatile leafy green vegetable best kept in the fridge.
Papaya: Both **green** and **ripe papaya** are used in Thai cooking so look closely at the recipe for which one you want as they are very different.
Pineapple and Juice: Pineapple is so much sweeter in Thailand and I love the way they sell it in carts on the street displayed on crushed ice and served in little bags with a dip of sugar and chilli powder and a stick to eat it with. It sounds bizarre but really works. If the recipe calls for pineapple juice a carton will suffice.
Pomelo: A pomelo is wonderful in a salad made with chilli jam but if you can't get it you could substitute with grapefruit.
Pumpkin: You can use any type of pumpkin to make the dishes in this book.
Shallots: The Thai shallot is very small and red but if you can't find it you can substitute with any other type.
Somsaa: I have never seen these sour oranges with green skin in the UK but you could substitute with blood orange or a mixture of tangerine juice and lime which is as close as you can get.
***Spinach:** Any type of spinach is fine to use.
***Spring Onions:** Very useful for salads or sliced to decorate a dish.
***Straw Mushrooms:** If you can't find these, replace with a firm chestnut mushroom or use canned.
***Tomato:** Small cherry tomatoes on the vine are best.
Young Kale Leaves: This superfood is becoming more widespread in the UK. Look for the young version as it can be too woody if it is old.

Suppliers I love and why.......... Carole X

www.theasiancookshop.co.uk
I love them because they do mail order and have a fantastic range of products.
They also group ingredients together by cookbook authors making it easy to buy what you want.

www.tawana.co.uk
I love them because they are really accessible in London near Bayswater Road, open really late and always have a good range of desserts.

www.wingyip.com
I love them because they have stores in Birmingham, Manchester, Croyden and Cricklewood and they have a great range of fresh fruit, vegetables and seafood that are hard to find elsewhere.
Most importantly they stock coriander root!

Curries

มัสมั่นไก่
100 บาท
หมูทอด
100 บาท
หมูจ๋า
เนื้อทอด
120บาท
ผัดฉ่าลูกชิ้นปลากราย
100 บาท
ผัดเผ็ดหมูป่า
120 บาท

Green Chicken Curry

Gaeng Gwiowan Gai

Green Curry Paste Ingredients:
10 green finger chillies, ends removed but with the seeds left in
5 birds eye chillies, ends removed but with the seeds left in
1 teaspoon of sea salt
1 teaspoon of galangal sliced
2 tablespoons of thinly sliced lemongrass
10 white peppercorns
1 teaspoon of scraped and chopped coriander root
2 tablespoons of garlic - use the small Thai version if you can get it
2 tablespoons of sliced shallots
2 teaspoons of coriander seeds - dry roasted and ground
1/2 teaspoon of cumin seeds - dry roasted and ground
1 teaspoon of shrimp paste dry roasted in the oven or refreshed in the microwave for a few seconds
Note: This curry can be made with any meat or fish but if Mae made it with beef or lamb she added a teaspoon of roasted and ground white peppercorns to this paste

Other Ingredients:
a batch of paste
250 - 400ml of coconut cream - see page 8 for instructions
250ml of coconut milk - see page 8 for instructions
250g of boneless chicken breasts sliced diagonally
2 tablespoons of fish sauce
1/2 teaspoon of palm sugar
a handful of pea aubergines taken off the stalks and added whole
4 apple aubergines quartered
3-4 kaffir lime leaves de-veined and torn
a handful of Thai basil
2 long red chillies sliced diagonally for serving

First make up a batch of the paste - see page 12 for instructions.

Make up the coconut milk and cream and put in the fridge - see page 8 for instructions.
Split the coconut cream by heating it in a heavy bottomed pan and boiling it over a medium heat for a few minutes until you can see the oil separating and rising to the top.
Fry all of the paste in the resulting coconut oil for five minutes until you can smell the dry spices developing.
Add the chicken and stir through well until the chicken starts to become opaque.
Add the fish sauce and then the coconut milk followed by the sugar then simmer until the chicken is cooked which will only take a few minutes.
Add the two types of aubergines, kaffir lime leaves and basil (saving a little for decoration) and simmer for a few minutes until the vegetables are cooked but still retain their crunch.

Transfer to a serving bowl and serve immediately using a bit of extra basil and the sliced red chillies to decorate. This dish is complimented by steamed jasmine rice.

Gaeng Pah

Jungle Curry

Jungle Curry Paste Ingredients:
10-12 small green chillies
a pinch of sea salt
1 chopped coriander root
2 tablespoons of finely sliced lemongrass
1 tablespoon of sliced shallots
1 tablespoon of sliced galangal
1 tablespoon of sliced garlic
1 teaspoon of coriander seeds dry roasted and ground
10 white peppercorns
1 teaspoon of shrimp paste refreshed for a few seconds in the microwave

Other Ingredients:
1 batch of paste - see page 12 for instructions
3 tablespoons of vegetable oil
300g of fish or boneless chicken sliced diagonally
1 tablespoon of fish sauce
3-4 cups of chicken or fish stock - see page 10 for instructions
5 pieces of small green apple aubergine
1 cup of snake beans cut into 3cm pieces
1 cup of bamboo shoots cut into 3cm pieces (if you used canned, wash them well)
1 tablespoon of peeled and shredded grachai
2 medium red and green chillies cut into fine strips
5 young green peppercorn strips washed and left whole
5 kaffir lime leaves de-veined and torn
1 cup of holy basil leaves washed and removed from the stems

To Decorate:
1 large red chilli cut into fine strips
Serve with a range of raw vegetables especially green beans

First make the paste and put to one side.
Heat the oil in a small pan and add the curry paste, stirring constantly for a few minutes until it produces a lovely aroma.

Add the chicken or fish and simmer until lightly cooked then season with fish sauce.

Heat the stock and add it to the pan and bring to a rolling boil.
Add the aubergine, snake beans and bamboo shoots then when they are almost cooked add the grachai, mixed chillies, green peppercorns, kaffir lime leaves and holy basil.
Taste and add more fish sauce if necessary and serve decorated with the red chilli slices.

Serve with a fresh raw vegetable salad especially including green beans which have been lightly cooked.

Penang Gung

Penang Prawn Curry

This dish is unusual in the way that it does not have the word "Geang" in the title which means curry. I asked Mae why and she explained that originally it was a very dry dish made with whole chicken. Over time it has morphed into a soupier curry with chopped meat making it more adaptable to everyday cooking.

Penang Paste Ingredients:
Note: If you make this paste for a meat or chicken version add 5 black peppercorns
6 long dried red chillies cut into 5cm pieces and soaked until soft then de-seeded
1/2 teaspoon of sea salt
3 scraped and chopped coriander roots
2 tablespoons of finely sliced lemongrass
2 teaspoons of galangal chopped
3 tablespoons of sliced shallots
1 teaspoon of kaffir lime zest - see glossary page 19
2 tablespoons of chopped garlic
1.5cm of cinnamon stick dry roasted and ground
2 teaspoons of coriander seeds dry roasted and ground
1/2 teaspoon of cumin seeds dry roasted and ground
2 teaspoons of shrimp paste dry roasted in the oven

Other Ingredients:
250ml of coconut cream - see page 8 for instructions
4 tablespoons of Penang paste
20 raw prawns peeled and de-veined with the tails left on
250ml of coconut milk - see page 8 for instructions
3 tablespoons of fish sauce
1 teaspoon of palm sugar
a large handful of Thai basil taken off the stalks and washed
3 large red chillies cut diagonally to decorate
4 finely shredded de-veined kaffir lime leaves to decorate

First make up a batch of the paste - see page 12 for instructions.
Put 1/2 cup of coconut cream in a pan on a medium heat and simmer until the oil rises to the top, this should take a few minutes. Reserve some of the cream for topping.
Add the curry paste and stir constantly for a few minutes until it produces a lovely aroma.
You should notice that at some point you will start to smell the dried spices and when you do then add the prawns and stir them into the paste.
Add in as much of the coconut milk as you need.
This should be quite a dry curry but it can be made moister to taste.
Heat through until the prawns are cooked. Note that this will be very fast so be careful not to overcook them as they will turn rubbery.
Finish off by adding the fish sauce and sugar, add gradually, tasting and adjusting until you get the correct balance.
Quickly stir through the basil.

Garnish with the finely shredded lime leaves and chilli and serve drizzled with a touch of coconut cream.

Gaeng Hang Lae

Chiang Mai Curry

Gaeng Hang Lae Paste Ingredients:
12 tablespoons of large dried red chillies cut into 5cm pieces, soaked till soft then de-seeded
3 tablespoons of lemongrass finely sliced
3 1/2 tablespoons of shallots finely sliced
3 tablespoons of garlic, sliced
2 tablespoons of Gaeng Hang Lae powder - see details on page 16
2 teaspoons of dry roasted shrimp paste

Other Ingredients:
a batch of paste as above - see page 12 for instructions
1 kilo of boneless pork rib washed and cut into 4cm cubes
1 kilo of pork belly washed and cut into 4cm cubes keeping the skin on
4 tablespoons of vegetable oil
300ml of chicken stock - see page 10 for instructions
500ml of water
1 teaspoon of table salt
4 tablespoons of fish sauce
3 1/2 tablespoons of tamarind juice
10 cloves of garlic - keep two on one side for later
16 tablespoons of shredded ginger
12 whole shallots peeled
2 tablespoons of palm sugar
35 cloves of pickled garlic - you will need a 150g jar and you will need to use the juice too
80ml of pickled garlic juice

First make up the Gaeng Hang Lae powder if necessary, then make up the paste - see page 12 for instructions.
Massage the paste into the pork ribs and allow this to marinate in the fridge for an hour.
Render the fat from the pork belly by dry frying the meat in a heavy bottomed pan, stirring and turning the meat occasionally. Make sure that the flame is not too high or you will burn the meat.
After 15 minutes add 4 tablespoons of vegetable oil and slowly cook until golden brown - this should take about 30 minutes.
Place both types of meat in a pan and slowly add the chicken stock ladle by ladle ensuring each addition is fully integrated as you add it. This allows the paste flavours to develop and emerge - if you add it all at once you will swamp the flavours of the paste. Bring to a boil.
Add the water, salt and fish sauce and simmer for 20 minutes.
Add the tamarind juice and then simmer for 2 hours stirring occasionally and topping up with a bit of water if you need to. You need to keep the meat covered with liquid.
Add 8 fresh whole garlic cloves, shredded ginger and the whole shallots.
Gradually add in the palm sugar. I find it easiest to take a spoonful of the curry and melt the sugar in that and then stir it in. Add the pickled garlic and its juice and the 2 fresh garlic cloves you reserved.
Simmer for another 10 minutes and you're ready!
This dish also keeps well so you can make it a day ahead if you like.
Serve with sticky rice.

Recipe
Serves Four

Chu Chi Talay

Fish and Coconut Curry

Chu Chi Paste Ingredients
5 large dried red chillies cut into 5cm pieces, soaked in water till soft then de-seeded
1/2 teaspoon of sea salt
2 coriander roots
2 tablespoons of lemongrass finely sliced
2 teaspoons of peeled galangal
2 tablespoons of sliced shallots
2 tablespoons of sliced garlic
2 teaspoons of dry fried and ground coriander seeds
1 teaspoon of shrimp paste dry fried

Other Ingredients:
1 1/2 cups of coconut cream - see page 8 for instructions
4 tablespoons of curry paste
300g of boneless white fish
3 tablespoons of fish sauce
1 teaspoon of palm sugar
4 kaffir lime leaves de-stemmed and finely shredded
2 handfuls of Thai sweet basil
2 large red chillies cut into fine slivers.

First make the curry paste - see page 12 for instructions.
Bring the coconut cream to a boil in a small pan and simmer until the oil separates out and rises to the top.
Keep a tablespoonful of the cream on one side to use as garnish.
Add the curry paste and cook, stirring constantly until the oil rises and you can start to smell the dried spices.
Put in the fish and gently stir through. It should cook very quickly so be careful not to overcook it.
Gradually add the fish sauce and palm sugar, adjusting the taste to balance.
Finally quickly stir through the lime leaves and basil.

Put on a serving plate and garnish with the strips of chilli and the reserved coconut cream.

To really impress your guests you could make the stuffed squid on page 107 and then use that to replace the fish in this dish x

Gaeng Ghari

Beef Curry Curry

Ning says that this funny name comes about because Gaeng means curry in Thai but when the Thai people tried to say curry at first it came out as Ghari and it stuck! This dish also works well with chicken.

Gaeng Ghari Paste Ingredients:

6 large dried red chillies cut into 5cm pieces, soaked in water until soft then de-seeded
a pinch of sea salt
1 tablespoon of finely sliced lemongrass
1 teaspoon of sliced galangal
1 teaspoon of chopped turmeric
1 teaspoon of fresh ginger sliced and dry fried
1 tablespoon of shallots sliced and dry fried
1 tablespoon of garlic sliced and dry fried
1 teaspoon of coriander seeds dry roasted and ground
a pinch of cumin seeds dry roasted and ground
2 white or green cardamom, seeds only
a pinch of ground cinnamon
1 tablespoon of Chinese curry powder
1 teaspoon of dry roasted shrimp paste

Other Ingredients:

A batch of paste
400ml of coconut milk - see page 8 for instructions
300ml of coconut cream - see page 8 for instructions
400g of beef steak cut into 5cm cubes
2 teaspoons of table salt
2 tablespoons of shallots sliced and deep fried
4 tablespoons of vegetable oil plus oil for deep frying
400g of potatoes cut into chunks
1-2 tablespoons of fish sauce

First make the paste and set aside - see page 12 for instructions.
Then make the coconut milk and cream - see page 8 for instructions.
Boil the beef in the coconut milk with the salt until it becomes tender.
Deep fry the shallots and set aside.
Put the 4 tablespoons of oil in a pan and fry the paste for a minute or two stirring continuously.
Start to add in the coconut cream bit by bit until it is all combined.
When fragrant add the cooked beef and poaching liquid and simmer until the beef is really tender.
Add in the potatoes and fish sauce tasting as you do this to make sure it is not too salty.
Simmer until the potatoes are cooked through but not breaking up.
Meanwhile make the cucumber relish (Ajad) to serve with this - see page 130.

Put the deep fried shallots on top of the curry and serve with the dip and steamed jasmine rice.

Gaeng Lueng

Yellow Fish Curry

Fresh turmeric is what gives this curry its vibrant yellow colour and this is often used in the South of Thailand which is a very rainy region. Mae explained that in Thailand they believe that eating very spicy food with turmeric counteracts the adverse effects of the rain on the body and so this dish energises you!

Yellow Curry Paste ingredients:
3 orange chillies chopped
2 tablespoons of large dried red chillies cut into 5cm pieces, soaked in water until soft then de-seeded
a pinch of sea salt
14 tablespoons of shallots sliced
2 tablespoons of garlic sliced
2 tablespoons of fresh turmeric sliced
2 tablespoons of raw shrimp boiled for ten minutes then pounded
2 teaspoons of dry roasted shrimp paste

Other Ingredients:
a batch of paste - see page 12 for instructions
4 cups of chicken stock - see page 10 for instructions
2 teaspoons of table salt
1 tablespoon of tamarind paste
4 tablespoons of fish sauce
5 kaffir lime leaves de-veined and torn
200g of fresh green papaya or canned bamboo shoots
200g of white fish or 12 big prawns peeled and de-veined

First make up a batch of the paste - see page 12 for instructions.
Put the stock in a small pan and bring to the boil.
Once it is at a rolling boil add the paste into the stock.
Season with salt, tamarind paste and fish sauce.
Tear the kaffir lime leaves and discard the central vein then add to the pot.
Add the vegetables and cook until they are cooked through.
If you are using the papaya it will take a while but if you are using the canned bamboo shoots this should be pretty quick.
Once cooked add the fish or prawns.
When the fish is cooked through then transfer to a serving bowl.
Serve with steamed jasmine rice.

This dish could also be made with chicken.

Gaeng Massaman Gai

Chicken Massaman Curry

Serves Four

Massaman Paste Ingredients:
7 tablespoons of large dried red chillies cut into 5cm pieces soaked in water until soft, then de-seeded
a pinch of sea salt
2 tablespoons of scraped and chopped coriander root
1/4 cup of thinly sliced lemongrass
1/4 cup of sliced shallots
1/4 cup of garlic sliced and dry roasted in the oven
2 teaspoons of galangal dry roasted in the oven
1 tablespoon of coriander seeds dry roasted and ground
1 teaspoon of cumin seeds dry roasted and ground
10 white cardamom pods firstly dry roasted in the oven and then the skin removed and only the seeds kept
if you can't get white cardamoms then use 5 green cardamoms instead
1/4 of a whole nutmeg dry roasted and ground
1/2 tablespoon of mace dry roasted and ground
1 teaspoon of cinnamon dry roasted and ground
8 cloves dry roasted and ground
1 teaspoon of white peppercorns dry roasted and ground
1 teaspoon of shrimp paste dry roasted in the oven

Other Ingredients:
vegetable oil for deep frying
1 kilo of chicken thighs on the bone
4 potatoes peeled and quartered
5 red shallots peeled
750ml of freshly made coconut cream - see page 8 for instructions
a batch of Massaman paste
2-3 tablespoons of fish sauce
2-3 tablespoons of tamarind paste
10 Thai cardamom pods or 5 green cardamom pods
10 bay leaves dry roasted in the oven
1 cup of pineapple juice
1/2 cup of palm sugar
a handful of unsalted roasted peanuts

First make the paste - see page 12 for instructions.
Prepare the ingredients, then one by one deep fry the chicken, potatoes and shallots and set aside.
Put 1/2 cup of coconut cream in a pan on a medium heat and simmer until the oil rises to the top, this should take a few minutes. Add the curry paste and stir constantly for a few minutes until it produces a lovely aroma.
I often feel that you start to smell the dried spices when it is ready also the oil rises to the top.
Season the sauce with the fish sauce and tamarind paste stirring constantly and cook for a minute.
Add the remaining coconut cream, cardamom pods and bay leaves.
Place the chicken thighs, potatoes and shallots in the sauce and simmer until the chicken is cooked and the sauce has reduced and thickened.
Finally stir in the pineapple juice and palm sugar and reheat.
Taste the curry, it should have a nice balance of sweet, sour and salty, and adjust to taste using extra tamarind and fish sauce if necessary. Add in the peanuts and serve once the peanuts have softened slightly.

This recipe is for four people, I made a big batch as it actually improves if it is left and reheated the next day.
You can also make a beef or lamb version of this curry.

Gaeng Kua Supporod

Red Curry with Prawns and Pineapple

This recipe also works really well with mussels and if you have any leftover red curry paste you can use it to make fishcakes.

Red Curry Paste Ingredients:
5 large dried red chillies cut into 5cm pieces, soaked in water until soft then de-seeded
a pinch of sea salt
1 teaspoon of scraped and chopped coriander root
1 teaspoon of galangal sliced
2 tablespoons of lemongrass peeled and thinly sliced
1 1/2 tablespoons of sliced garlic - use the small Thai version if you can
2 tablespoons of sliced shallots
1 teaspoon of shrimp paste dry roasted or refreshed for a few seconds in the microwave
2 tablespoons of dried shrimp

Other Ingredients:
300ml of coconut cream - see page 8 for instructions
red curry paste as above
300g of raw prawns peeled and de-veined
2 cups of pineapple cut into triangular chunks
3-4 tablespoons of fish sauce
2 teaspoons of palm sugar
3-4 tablespoons of tamarind paste
6 kaffir lime leaves de-veined and finely shredded - optional

First make the paste and put to one side - see page 12 for instructions.

Pour 1/2 cup of coconut cream in a pan on a medium heat and simmer until the oil rises to the top, this should take a few minutes.
Add the curry paste and stir constantly until it produces a lovely aroma.
I often feel that you start to smell the dry spices when it is ready and you will see pockets of red oil rise to the top.

Continue adding the coconut cream, a little at a time, and keep stirring until it is mixed in well. You should not add it all at once otherwise you will overwhelm the flavours in the paste.
Add the prawns and pineapple to the curry and bring back to the boil.
Season with fish sauce, palm sugar and tamarind paste and adjust to taste before serving. Top with finely shredded kaffir lime leaves.

龍蓮寺大雄寶殿

Gaeng Som

Prawn and Papaya Curry

This is a soupy style of curry that is extreme in its taste and it's not necessarily to the western palate. I was confused by the name Gaeng Som as Gaeng means curry, but I always thought of this as a soup. This dish serves as the sour element in a balanced meal of salty, sour, hot and sweet. It works well as a foil to a very hot dish or even to support simple fried fish or deep fried puffy omelette. It's great to compliment Muu Parlow see page 48.

Gaeng Som Paste Ingredients:
5 tablespoons large dried red chillies cut into 5cm pieces, soaked in water until soft then de-seeded
2 cups of sliced shallots
4 tablespoons of sea bass or white fish de-boned and grilled or dry fried
4 teaspoons of shrimp paste dry fried or refreshed in the microwave for a few seconds
a pinch of sea salt

Other Ingredients:
3 cups of chicken stock - see page 10 for instructions
1 teaspoon of table salt
a batch of paste
1 cup of papaya and 1 cup of morning glory
or replace them with any one of these vegetables-
savoy cabbage - string beans - cauliflower - daikon
2 tablespoons of fish sauce
5 raw prawns washed, peeled and de-veined but keep the tails on
1/2 tablespoon of white sugar - I have put this as a guideline but use as little as possible
3 tablespoons of thick tamarind juice
2 eggs (if you are making the omelette)

First make up the paste - see page 12 for instructions.
Prepare all the vegetables.
Heat the stock until it comes to a rolling boil then add the salt and paste.
Add the vegetables and simmer until cooked but still firm.
Add the fish sauce and simmer until the aroma changes and it smells cooked.
Add prawns and cook briefly until the prawns turn pink, do not overcook them or they will be tough.
Reduce the heat and season with the sugar and tamarind juice, taste then add more fish sauce if it is needed.

Serve with an omelette. Use about 4 tablespoons of oil for 2 eggs and after whisking drop the egg mixture from shoulder height into the oil to get a frothy finish. Flip and serve.

Gaeng Ped Bed Yang

Roast Duck Curry with Pineapple

Paste Ingredients:
3 tablespoons of large dried red chillies cut into 5cm pieces, soaked in water until soft, then de-seeded
a pinch of sea salt
2 teaspoons of sliced galangal
1 1/2 tablespoons of finely sliced lemongrass
1 teaspoon of kaffir lime zest - see glossary page 19
2 coriander roots scraped
1 tablespoon of sliced garlic
1 tablespoon of sliced shallots
1 teaspoon of dry roasted shrimp paste
1 teaspoon of coriander seeds dry roasted and ground
a pinch of cumin seeds dry roasted and ground
a pinch of aromatic ginger (proh horm in Thai) - see glossary page 16
a pinch of cloves dry roasted and ground
a pinch of mace dry roasted and ground
a pinch of cinnamon stick dry roasted and ground
a pinch of ground white peppercorn

Other ingredients:
300ml of coconut cream - see page 8 for instructions
a batch of curry paste as above
400g of roasted boneless duck breast sliced on the diagonal
2 1/2 tablespoons of fish sauce
300ml of coconut milk - see page 8 for instructions
1/4 cup of pineapple cut into triangular chunks
1/4 cup of pea aubergines removed from stems and washed
2 kaffir lime leaves de-veined and torn into 4 pieces
a pinch of palm sugar
1/2 cup of sweet basil leaves
3 large red chillies cut into strips

First make the paste and put to one side - see page 12 for instructions.
Put the coconut cream in a pan on a medium heat and simmer until the oil rises to the top, this should take a few minutes.
Add the curry paste and stir constantly until it produces a lovely aroma and you start to smell the dried spices. When it is ready the oil will rise to the top.
Add the sliced duck and season with fish sauce and bring to a simmer.
Add the coconut milk gradually followed by the pineapple, pea aubergine and torn kaffir lime leaves.
Taste and add some palm sugar if needed.
Remove from the heat and quickly stir in the sweet basil leaves.
Decorate with a few extra basil leaves and the red chillies and serve with steamed jasmine rice.

This is a great dish to make with takeaway cooked Chinese duck.
There are a couple of ingredients in the paste that are not easy to get so I hesitated to put them in however it is worth the extra effort to seek them out, as actually they really make the curry sing.
If you have any spare cooked duck you could use it to make the rice pancakes on page 138.

Tom Yam Gung

Hot and Sour Prawn Soup

500ml of chicken stock - see page 10 for instructions
4 tablespoons of galangal sliced into rings
4 tablespoons of lemongrass sliced on the diagonal into 5cm pieces
8 quartered straw mushrooms or any firm mushrooms
12 raw prawns washed, peeled and de-veined
3 tablespoons of fish sauce
12 lime leaves
2 birds eye chillies bruised with a pestle and mortar
3 tablespoons of lime juice
4 tablespoons of coriander leaves chopped

Bring the stock to the boil in a small pan over a medium heat.
Add the galangal and lemongrass and bring back to the boil.

Add the mushrooms and prawns then when the prawns turn pink, which will be very quickly, add the fish sauce to the soup.

Tear the veins from the lime leaves and add the torn leaves to the pan with the bruised chillies.

Remove from the heat and add in the lime juice, gradually but do not add it all as the strength of fish sauce and lime juice varies every time.

Taste and adjust using extra fish sauce if needed to get the right balance of flavours between the lime juice and the fish sauce.

Ladle the soup into small bowls and garnish with the coriander leaves.

Soups

Muu Parlow

Pork and Egg Soup

This soup keeps a long time and in fact improves overnight so it's handy to have around for the family to help themselves to and as it is not spicy it's really comforting..

vegetable oil for deep frying
700g of belly pork cut into 2.5cm cubes
350g of beancurd or firm tofu washed and cut into 4cm cubes
10 white peppercorns
4 coriander roots scraped
a pinch of sea salt
5 garlic cloves peeled
3 tablespoons of vegetable oil
2 whole star anise
1 cinnamon stick
2 tablespoons of palm sugar
2 tablespoons of fish sauce
1 litre of chicken stock - see page 10 for instructions
2 tablespoons of dark soy sauce
6 hard boiled eggs peeled
a handful of chopped coriander leaves

Cube and deep fry the pork belly in batches and put to one side to drain.
Cube and deep fry the bean-curd till crispy and put on one side to drain.

Pound the white peppercorns then add the coriander roots with a pinch of salt and pound again.
Once integrated, add the garlic cloves and pound until the paste is complete.

Shallow fry the resultant paste in 3 tablespoons of oil, adding in the star anise and cinnamon.
It is important not to burn the paste but cook it until it is golden brown.
Add the sugar and fish sauce and stir until the sugar has melted.
Add the stock and soy sauce followed by the meat.
Simmer for at least an hour and a half until the meat is really well cooked.
Add the whole boiled eggs and beancurd and simmer for 10 minutes.

Top tip - Put 5 whole garlic cloves and a knob of ginger in when you finish the dish and allow these to stand but remember to discard them before serving!
When ready to serve, reheat, put into a large bowl and sprinkle with coriander leaves.

Serves Four

Tom Saep

Sour Pork Rib Soup

500ml of water
a pinch of table salt
200g of pork rib on the bone
500ml of chicken stock - see page 10 for instructions
1 stalk of lemongrass sliced
2 slices of galangal
1 coriander root
2 kaffir lime leaves de-veined and torn
4 tablespoons of fish sauce
3 tablespoons of tamarind juice
2 teaspoons of chilli powder
a handful of chopped mint or sawtooth coriander
2 tablespoons of dry fried rice
2 spring onions chopped into 5cm pieces
3 sliced shallots

Gently heat the water and a pinch of salt in a small pan and boil the ribs for 20 minutes.
Drain the ribs and put aside.

Put the chicken stock in a pan along with lemongrass, galangal and coriander root.

Bring to the boil then add the ribs and boil gently for twenty minutes or until the ribs are tender.
Drop in the torn lime leaves.
Season with fish sauce, tamarind and dried chilli powder, adding them all cautiously testing as you go.
Remove the pan from the heat and add the mint or sawtooth coriander.

Pour into a serving bowl or bowls and lastly sprinkle with the dry fried rice, spring onions and shallots.

In Issan saep means delicious and that describes this soup perfectly.
Don't let it sit around or reheat it as it will turn salty and sour !

Good Old Fashioned Soup

Paste Ingredients:
2 teaspoons of whole white peppercorns
a pinch of sea salt
1/4 cup of dried shrimp
1/4 cup of sliced shallots
a teaspoon of dry roasted shrimp paste

Other Ingredients:
250ml of vegetable stock - see page 10 for instructions
a pinch of table salt
1/2 cup pumpkin peeled and cubed
a batch of paste as above
1/2 cup of mushrooms, straw mushrooms ideally but if not choose a nice firm mushroom
1 cup of gourd peeled and cut into triangle shapes
1/2 cup of raw prawns peeled and de-veined but leave the tails on
1 cup of spinach - the Thais use a kind of spinach that looks like Ivy but we rarely get it in the UK so you can substitute with any spinach
fish sauce to taste
1 cup of lemon basil - leaves removed and washed

Make the paste by pounding the white peppercorns and salt then add the dried shrimp and pound again.
When completely pounded add the shallots and pound till integrated.
Finally pound in the shrimp paste then mix well with a metal spoon at the end.

Prepare all the vegetables.
Heat the stock until it comes to a rolling boil then add the salt.
Add the pumpkin and cook until cooked but still firm.
Add the paste and simmer until the aroma changes and it smells cooked.
Add the mushroom and gourd to the soup and boil for 1 minute.
Add prawns and spinach and cook briefly until the prawns turn pink.
Season with fish sauce then add the lemon basil and quickly remove from the stove and serve.

Gang Jude

Pork Ball Soup

1 tablespoon of dried shrimp
1 teaspoon of whole white peppercorns
1 tablespoon of coriander root
1 teaspoon of sea salt
1 teaspoon of chopped garlic
400g of minced pork - chopped with a cleaver from 20% fatty pork
1 tablespoon of cornflour
500ml of chicken stock - see page 10 for instructions
2 carrots sliced in rounds with a shaped edge if you have time
a handful of straw mushrooms halved
1-2 tablespoons of light soy sauce
a pinch of white sugar (optional)
spring onion 1/4 cup cut into 5cm strips
Chinese celery 1/4 cup cut into 5cm strips
1/4 cup of chopped coriander leaves

In a pestle and mortar pound the dried shrimp until it is a fine powder then add in the white peppercorns, coriander root, the salt and garlic and pound until you have a smooth paste.

Massage the paste with the pork and flour and roll into 2.5cm balls.

Boil the stock and cook the carrots in it for five minutes.

Add the mushrooms and cook for another two minutes.

Drop in the balls and boil until the pork is cooked.

Remove from the heat and add the soy sauce and sugar.

Quickly stir in the spring onions, Chinese celery and coriander leaves and transfer to a serving bowl.

Khao Tom Muu

Ning tells me that every Thai family has their own version of this soup so I decided to put in the Mason family recipe..We have this the morning after every Thai dinner party whilst the ingredients are around as we have invariably drunk too much the night before and have a mountain of washing up to face..We think it helps us to feel better able to cope with the work but perhaps we have just found a tasty way of putting it off...

12 shallots sliced and deep fried till golden for the topping
10 cloves of garlic chopped and deep fried till golden for the topping
5 white peppercorns
a pinch of sea salt
3 coriander roots scraped
3 garlic cloves
200g of pork or chicken
50g of raw prawns
500ml of chicken stock - see page 10 for instructions
1 1/2 tablespoons of light soy sauce
1 1/2 tablespoons of fish sauce
2 cups of cooked rice
2 tablespoons of coarsely chopped coriander
1 lightly whisked egg
dried chilli flakes to serve

Deep fry the shallots and garlic and set aside.
Make a paste by pounding the white peppercorns, salt, coriander roots and garlic in a pestle and mortar.
Mince the prawns and chicken together by hand with a cleaver and add the mixture into the mortar and massage in with your hands.
Bring the chicken stock to a rolling boil in the pan, form the meat and prawn mixture into rough balls and drop in one by one.

In a few minutes, when they have cooked, season with the soy and fish sauce.
Taste and adjust - the soy and fish sauce should taste balanced, one should not overwhelm the other.
Put in the cooked rice and stir well to ensure that the rice breaks up.
Remove from the heat and quickly stir in the coriander leaves.

Put the whisked egg in large cold serving bowl.
When the soup has cooled a little ladle it on top. If you do not allow the soup to cool first the egg will turn into omelette.
I know it seems weird to have raw egg in the soup but it really does soften it and change the taste.

Ladle into individual serving bowls and top each bowl with the shallots and garlic.
Serve with dried chilli flakes and fish sauce so that everyone can decide how hot and salty they want it for themselves.
Do not allow this soup to stand after it has been made otherwise the rice expands and it becomes gooey.

Carole's Hangover Cure!

Tom Kloang

Fish and Vegetable Soup

This soup has an extensive ingredient list and you need to have the BBQ running to make it but if you're already grilling it is actually quite quick to make.

BBQ the following ingredients and put on one side to cool and when cooled discard the skins
1 tablespoon of galangal
1 tablespoon of lemongrass
1 tablespoon of garlic cloves whole with the skin on
1 tablespoon of shallots whole with the skin on
1 cup of white fish

Other Ingredients:
500ml of water
1/2 cup mushrooms sliced
1 tablespoon of fish sauce
3 kaffir lime leaves
5 medium green fresh chillies
1 tablespoon of coriander leaves
1 tablespoon of spring onions chopped into 5cm pieces
1 tablespoon of chopped sawtooth coriander
1 tablespoon of lime juice
5 large dried chillies deep fried for decoration

First prepare and BBQ all the ingredients as above list, allow them to cool and when cooled discard the skins.

In a small pan bring the water to a boil and add the mushrooms, galangal and lemongrass. Add the fish and season with fish sauce.

Add the BBQ'd garlic and shallots to the pan.

Bruise the chillies with a pestle and mortar and add to the soup.

Reduce the heat and add the chopped coriander, spring onion and sawtoothed coriander. Finally put the lime juice in the shared serving bowl and ladle the soup into that.

Garnish with the deep fried chillies and serve immediately.

Tom Ka Gai

Chicken Coconut and Galangal Soup

This is the classic soup that we all know and love and it is surprisingly easy and fast to cook
It also works well with prawns or seafood but you really need to make it with fresh coconut milk
as the canned variety is just too thick for soup.
I'm sure it will become a firm favourite in your kitchen.

500ml of chicken stock - see page 10 for instructions
2 tablespoons of galangal chopped into thin rounds
1 stalk of lemongrass sliced into 2 inch pieces on the diagonal
125g of chicken breast sliced diagonally
1 cup of straw mushrooms quartered - if you can't get straw mushrooms choose a firm mushroom
2 tablespoons of fish sauce
4 kaffir lime leaves stems de-veined and torn
8 birds eye chillies bruised with a pestle and mortar
10 tablespoons of coconut cream - see page 8 for instructions
2 tablespoons of lime juice

Gently heat the stock in a small pan. Please make your own stock for this it will make the world of difference!

Once it begins to boil add the galangal and simmer for a minute.
Now add the lemongrass and simmer for another minute.

Drop in the chicken and mushrooms and season with fish sauce as soon as the chicken turns opaque and is just cooked.

Tear the kaffir lime leaves and add to the pot and reduce the heat.

Add the bruised chillies.

Ladle the coconut cream into the simmering pot and cook until it just starts to show a light creamy texture.
Do not overcook it as you do not want it to be too creamy and thick or the chicken will turn rubbery.
Remove from the heat.

Divide the lime juice between the serving bowls and ladle the soup on top of it.

Serve immediately.
Don't let this soup sit around or reheat it after you have made it as it will turn salty and sour.

Tom Som Sapporat

Sour Pineapple Soup Mae Style

Paste Ingredients:
10 white peppercorns
1/2 cup of dried shrimp
a pinch of sea salt
2 shallots
3 coriander roots
1/2 teaspoon of root ginger
3/4 teaspoon dry roasted shrimp paste

Other Ingredients:
500ml of chicken stock - see page 10 for instructions
25g of cooked chicken - shredded

If you don't have any cooked chicken to hand then season some flattened chicken breast with fish sauce and grill or dry fry it.

500g of pineapple chopped into bite sized pieces
2 tablespoons of fish sauce
1 tablespoon of deep fried dried shrimp
2 tablespoons of chives

First make the paste by pounding the white peppercorns in a pestle and mortar followed by the dried shrimp and salt.

Add the shallots and pound fully into the paste. Then repeat this process with the coriander root and finally the ginger. Do not add another ingredient until you are satisfied that the last one is fully pounded in.
Finally stir in the shrimp paste.

Gently heat the stock in a small pan then add the paste and simmer for five minutes.

Add the chicken and pineapple and bring back to the boil and warm through.

Remove from the heat and add the fish sauce.

Put into serving bowls and top with the dried shrimp and chives and serve immediately.

Tom Som Saparot is an old fashioned soup rarely seen outside the home.
It was traditionally made with pork belly but this was Mae's favourite way to prepare it.
The taste is very close to Tom Som yet the tiny amount of shrimp paste in this recipe makes it different.
It's still fishy but the dried shrimp adds a deeper dimension and so the overall effect is changed.

Tom Jude Tung Galamplee

Pork and Prawn Parcel Soup

Paste Ingredients:
10 whole white peppercorns
5 coriander roots scraped
2 cloves of peeled garlic
a pinch of sea salt

Other Ingredients:
150g of pork - choose pork with some fat in - it it should not be too lean
8 raw prawns - washed, peeled and de-veined
1 teaspoon of cornflour
1 tablespoon of light soy sauce
white only from half an egg
12 cabbage or spinach leaves
chives for tying the parcels or replace with strips of banana leaf or pandanus leaf
500ml of chicken stock - see page 10 for instructions
2 tablespoons of fish sauce

With a heavy cleaver combine and mince the pork and prawn chopping it repeatedly until you have a finely combined mince adding a pinch of salt as you go along then put to one side.

In a pestle and mortar make a paste by pounding the white peppercorns, coriander roots, garlic and a pinch of salt.

Mix the paste with the meat and prawn mixture then add the cornflour and soy sauce and put on one side to marinate for thirty minutes.

Gradually add in the egg white using as much as you need to get a firm consistency but do not make the mixture too runny.

Fill the cabbage or spinach leaves with stuffing and secure with the chives.

Heat the chicken stock in a small pan and drop the parcels into the simmering broth.
Simmer until the meat and prawns are cooked through.

Remove the pan from the heat and add the fish sauce and serve immediately.

Photo taken at
Wat Chanasongkhram
a hidden treasure
opposite
Khao San Road

Thai Chilli Jam is Amazing!

The recipe on page 66 in this chapter is a great addition to your Thai armoury.

Although it takes some time and effort to make it, once it's made it keeps in the fridge for months and enables you to whip up many quick and tasty dishes.

I have put several recipes in various sections of this book so that once you have some made you will find it easy to make up some wonderful meals with it.

The recipes are:

Pomelo Salad page 68
Wing Bean Salad page 72
Banana Blossom Salad page 76
Stir Fried Mussels with Chilli Jam page 88
Stir Fried Seafood with Curry Paste page 101
Spicy Deep Fried Vegetables with Chilli Jam page 160

Carole X

Salads

Nahm Prik Pao

Thai Chilli Jam

vegetable oil for deep frying
1/2 cup of garlic sliced, washed and dried
1/2 cups of shallots sliced, washed and dried
1 cup of dried shrimp washed and soaked for twenty minutes then left to dry for an hour in a warm place or ideally overnight
1 tablespoon of shrimp paste dry roasted
15 dried red chillies - prepare the chillies by discarding the ends and cutting into 5cm pieces then soak in water until they are soft, de-seed and dry with paper towels or leave to dry overnight
3 tablespoons of tamarind pulp made up into a thick paste and sieved
1/2 cup of palm sugar
3 tablespoons of fish sauce - use shrimp paste if you like a fishier taste
1/2 teaspoon of table salt

One by one deep fry the garlic and shallots followed by the dried shrimp until golden brown.

Deep fry the chillies at a low temperature stirring all the time just for a minute or two, do not allow them to burn and allow for the fact that they will continue cooking for a while after you remove them.
You must fry the chillies last as they turn the oil black and then the ingredients you fry after could be tainted by this.

In a pestle and mortar pound the dried chillies very finely then one by one incorporate the garlic, shallots and finally the shrimp. Make sure you have incorporated all of one ingredient before moving to the next. Finally pound and stir in the shrimp paste.

Briefly fry the paste in a couple of tablespoons of oil, taken from the deep frying, in a heavy bottomed pan and after a couple of minutes add the tamarind, palm sugar, fish sauce and salt.

Bring slowly to the boil and simmer for five minutes stirring continuously.

Remove the pan from the heat and allow to cool.

Store in an airtight glass jar in the fridge for up to a month.

Yam Som O

Pomelo Salad

Pomelos are popping up in the UK more often these days but if you can't lay your hands on one you could substitute with grapefruit which is pretty similar, albeit more sour.

8 raw prawns
1 whole peeled and segmented pomelo
4 cups of vegetable oil
3-4 red chillies
1 cup of sliced garlic
3 large coriander roots
2 tablespoons of fish sauce
2 tablespoons of chilli jam see page 66
1 cup of sliced shallots
1 cup of dried shrimp
3 tablespoons of coconut cream - I often cheat and use canned because it is difficult to get fresh coconut cream to be thick enough in the UK
1/2 teaspoon of table salt

Peel and de-vein the prawns but leave a couple unpeeled to decorate the top of the salad with if you like. Steam or boil them until they turn pink. Do not overcook them or they become tough.

Peel and segment the pomelo. Break into small pieces and set aside - make sure you carefully remove all the white pith as it can be very bitter.

One by one deep fry the garlic, shallots and dried shrimp and set aside.

Pound the chillies, garlic and coriander root in a pestle and mortar.

Add some of the fish sauce and all of the chilli jam. Do not add all the fish sauce immediately, test it before you add it all as it depends how salty the chilli jam is as to whether you want it all in.

Finally stir in the coconut cream.

Combine all the ingredients and the sauce, add the salt, and toss gently before placing in a serving bowl. Be careful not to break up the pomelo when stirring.

Another Thai chilli jam delight!

Nahm Tok Muu

Northeastern Esarn Salad

Pork Marinade:
1 tablespoon of fish sauce
1 1/2 tablespoons of light soy sauce

Other Ingredients:
250g of pork (or you could use beef)
choose a couple of fresh raw vegetables - you can use anything you like here
half a cucumber
a handful of sweet basil

Sauce Ingredients:
1/2 a cup of chicken stock - see page 10 for instructions
5 shallots sliced
1 1/2 tablespoons of coriander leaves
1 1/2 tablespoons of chopped spring onions
2 tablespoons of lime juice
1 tablespoon of fish sauce
2 teaspoons of chilli flakes
1 1/2 tablespoons of mint
2 teaspoons of ground dry roast sticky rice - see page 11 for instructions

Marinate the meat with the fish sauce and light soy.
It is ideal to leave the marinade overnight but an hour minimum would be ok.

Next BBQ or grill the meat and leave it to rest for five minutes. Slice finely on the diagonal across the grain. If you are using pork cook it well but if you are using beef leave it quite rare.

To make the sauce, heat the chicken stock in a pan and add in all the other ingredients except the dry fried rice and mint. Season to taste, it should be salty, sour and spicy.

Add the sliced meat and stir well.

Remove from the heat and put into a bowl. Finish with the dry rice powder and mint.

Serve with the fresh raw vegetables, cucumber and sweet basil leaves.

Here I give a guideline of how much fish sauce, lime juice and chilli powder you should use but as these items and your taste vary so much you should pay close attention to tasting and adjusting them. The only rule is that one flavour should not overpower the other. X

Yam Tua Plu

Wing Bean Salad

I put this recipe in which is ideal to make with wing beans but actually it would work well with any beans.

250g of wing beans
100g of pork minced by hand with a cleaver
6 raw prawns peeled and de-veined
4 tablespoons of coconut cream - canned would be OK to use for this or see page 8
2-4 tablespoons of chilli jam see page 66 for recipe
2 tablespoons of sliced shallots
2 tablespoons of fish sauce
1/2 teaspoon of sugar
a pinch of table salt
2-3 tablespoons of lime juice
2 tablespoons of coconut shredded and roasted by dry frying or oven baking
2 tablespoons of peanuts roasted and pounded
2 hard boiled eggs peeled and cut into quarters to serve as an accompaniment

Blanch the wing beans in boiling water then refresh in cold water and set aside.
After mincing with a cleaver either briefly boil the pork and prawns or fry them without oil until cooked and put to one side.

Heat the coconut cream in a small pan stirring constantly so that the oil does not separate out. When it comes to the boil stir in the chilli jam.

Add in half of the shallots followed by the pork and prawn. Lower the heat and stir gently to combine them.

Season with fish sauce, sugar and a pinch of salt and remove from the heat.

Gently stir in the wing beans, season with the lime juice then add in the peanuts.

Add in half of the roasted coconut and gently stir to combine.

Display on a large plate and garnish with the boiled eggs, remaining shallots and toasted coconut.

It is especially important to taste this dish as you go, it should taste spicy, salty, sour and a little bit sweet. As fish sauce and limes always vary in taste the problem of giving precise quantities of each always exists but when you add the the extra element of chilli jam then finding the right balance of taste is crucial.

Yam Makrua

BBQ Aubergine Salad

The aubergines should ideally be barbecued but if you have a gas flame you can roast them, fed onto metal skewers, on the open flame.
When they are ready the juices will start to bubble out of the ends of the skewers.

4 tablespoons of pork - minced with a cleaver
a cup of chicken stock - see page 10 for instructions
8 raw prawns either BBQ'd then peeled or de-veined and boiled
2 long green aubergines - grill, allow to cool then peel
you could use the red aubergines we get in the UK as a replacement
vegetable oil for deep frying
4 tablespoons of shallots sliced and deep fried
2 tablespoons of grated coconut dry fried or oven baked
4 tablespoons of dried shrimp pounded in a pestle and mortar
coriander leaves to trim

Sauce Ingredients:
4 tablespoons of chicken stock - see page 10 for instructions
8 tablespoons of palm sugar
4 tablespoons of fish sauce
4 tablespoons of lime juice
2-4 birds eye chillies ends removed and crushed in a pestle and mortar
1 tablespoon of fried shallots

Cook the pork in the chicken stock and set aside.
BBQ the prawns and then peel and de-vein them.
BBQ the aubergine, and allow to cool before peeling off the blackened skin and cutting into large chunks.

Deep fry the shallots, grate and roast the coconut and pound the dried shrimp in a pestle and mortar and put to one side.

Mix all the sauce ingredients together and stir until the sugar has dissolved. If the sugar is hard heat it for a few seconds in a microwave before you put it in the sauce.

Gently stir in the minced pork, prawns and aubergine as you do not want the aubergine to completely fall apart.

Serve garnished with the deep fried shallots, toasted coconut, dried shrimp and coriander leaves.

Yam Hua Plee

Banana Blossom Salad

1 banana blossom or you can use canned
juice of one lime plus a tablespoon
1 teaspoon of table salt
1 tablespoon of palm sugar
1/2 cup of coconut cream - thick and fresh ideally - see page 8 for instructions or use canned
3 tablespoons of chilli jam - see recipe page 66
2 tablespoons of sliced red shallots
2 tablespoons of finely sliced lemongrass
1 cup of shredded green mango (use less if the mango is very sour)
300g of cooked chicken - ideally shredded BBQ'd chicken but you could use any cooked meat
1 tablespoon of fish sauce
coriander leaves and sweet basil - to garnish
3 birds eye chillies bruised

First make the chilli jam see page 66

Peel the banana blossom, discard the yellow stems, and stamen. Slice into small pieces on the diagonal and soak in water with the juice of 1 lime and a teaspoon of salt. - Do not do this too far ahead of time (20 minutes maximum) or the leaves will turn black.
Try and keep a good looking outer leaf to serve the salad in.
Boil a pot of water and drop the banana blossom in for for 2 minutes then drain. This softens it and turns it a darker colour.

In a separate pan melt the sugar in the coconut cream and add the chilli jam and salt and cook gently for a minute.
Take off the heat and add the shallots and lemongrass to the pan and stir well.
Transfer to a non metallic bowl and season with the tablespoon of lime juice and fish sauce to taste.
Gently stir in the mango and chicken - reserving a little of the mango for trimming.
Taste and adjust the seasoning as necessary.

Serve warm, at room temperature or cold but however you choose to eat it do not put it in the fridge or it will stiffen.

Garnish with the coriander leaves, sweet basil and chillies.

Dazzle your friends by serving it in a leaf and propping it up with a vegetable!

*This was the first thing I cooked with Mae and its still my favourite.
Banana blossoms are a gorgeous crimson colour and have tightly packed leaves,
their texture is similar to globe artichoke and it makes a good substitute.. Carole X*

Kanom Jeen Sao Nahm

Pineapple and Coconut Noodle Salad

4 cups of coconut milk- see page 8 for instructions
1/2 teaspoon of table salt
2 cups of Kanom Jeen noodles or any thin noodles
2 cups of diced pineapple
1 cup of peeled and shredded ginger
1 cup of garlic sliced lengthways
1 cup of pounded dried prawns
1 teaspoon of sugar
2 medium red chillies sliced
1 lime cut into small wedges

Put the coconut milk in a pan with the salt and bring to the boil then remove from the heat.
Cook the noodles as necessary according to the manufacturers instructions, blanch in cold water and put into a bowl.

Arrange all the other ingredients in individual serving bowls.

To serve take two individual bowls and place some noodles in them.

Pour the coconut milk on top and garnish with the pineapple, ginger, garlic, dried shrimp and chilli and sprinkle some sugar on top to taste.

Top with the wedges of lime and adjust the saltiness with fish sauce if required.

Yam Pla Too

Mackerel Salad

In Thailand little mackerel are sold pre steamed in baskets in every market. It may be possible for you to buy some from the freezer in oriental shops but if not just buy mackerel and steam it yourself.

Ingredients:

vegetable oil for deep frying
2 cups of mackerel
4 tablespoons of fish sauce
3 tablespoons of lime juice
4 tablespoons of lemongrass finely sliced
2 tablespoons of birds eye chillies finely sliced
1 cup of chopped spring onions
1 cup of sliced shallots
1 cup of sliced ginger
2 teaspoons of caster sugar
6 tablespoons of coarsely chopped mint leaves

If you are using fresh mackerel steam until cooked and set aside.

Once cooked skin and de-bone the fish, cut it into pieces and deep fry.

Mix the fish sauce and lime juice in a bowl and add all the ingredients including the fish except for the mint.

Gently stir together.

Serve on a platter garnished with the mint.

Larb Mueng

Northern Larb with Sticky Rice

Powder Ingredients:
2 teaspoons of ground coriander seeds
2 tablespoons of makwaen pepper
2 tablespoons of fennel seeds
2 tablespoons of malhap
20 pieces of long pepper
1/2 tablespoon of black peppercorns
5 cloves
1 tablespoon of ground star anise
2 tablespoons of pro horm
1/2 teaspoon of nutmeg
1/2 teaspoon of mace
1/2 teaspoon of ground cinnamon
1 tablespoon of white cardamom seeds only
1 teaspoon of table salt

**Grind all the powder ingredients in a coffee grinder and store in a glass jar for future use -
this makes approx 10 tablespoons**

Paste Ingredients:
9 small dried red chillies dry fried
1 teaspoon of galangal dry fried
2 tablespoons of lemongrass dry fried
2 tablespoons of shallots dry fried
1/4 cup of garlic dry fried
1 tablespoon of the powder

Other Ingredients:
350g of beef or pork minced by hand with a chopper
2 tablespoons of vegetable oil
3 tablespoons of spring onions chopped into rounds
2 tablespoons of fish sauce
3 tablespoons of chopped coriander leaves
1 tablespoon of sliced shallots
juice of 1 lime
1/4 cup of garlic chopped and deep fried for topping
raw vegetables to serve as a salad
sticky rice to serve

Make up the powder and put to one side.

To make the paste dry fry the chillies, galangal, lemongrass, shallots and garlic, allow to cool and then pound in a pestle and mortar before stirring in the tablespoon of powder.

Chop the meat with a cleaver and then stir into the paste.

Fry the meat in the oil until cooked then add half of the spring onions and season with the fish sauce.

Remove from the heat and add in the coriander, remaining spring onions and the shallots - reserving a few to sprinkle on top.

Finally squeeze in the lime juice.

Sprinkle with the deep fried garlic and sliced shallots and serve with a raw vegetable salad and sticky rice.

You can make the paste for this and keep it in the fridge then put it together really quickly and serve with rice..

Larb Mueng is usually enjoyed in the north of Thailand without lime juice but Mae loved to flavour her dish this way..

Larb Muu

Spicy Pork Salad

300g of pork or chicken minced by hand with a cleaver
1-2 cups of chicken stock - see page 10 for instructions
2 tablespoons of fish sauce
3 tablespoons of lime juice
2 teaspoons of chilli flakes
2 tablespoons of roasted ground sticky rice - see page 11 for details
2 tablespoons of sliced spring onions
4 tablespoons of shallots
1 handful of mint leaves
2 tablespoons of chopped coriander leaves
1/2 cabbage cut into chunks
a handful of green beans washed and cut into 3 inch lengths

Cook the pork or chicken in the stock stirring constantly for a few minutes until it is cooked.
Drain, then season with fish sauce.
Season with the lime juice and chilli flakes and mix well. Taste and adjust the fish sauce and lime juice if necessary.
Add the ground rice, spring onions, shallots, mint and coriander.
Transfer to a serving plate and serve with raw cabbage and beans.

Goong Chae Nham Pla

Prawn and Bitter Melon Canapé

This is the most wonderful and simple canapé.

6 raw prawns
a small amount of bitter melon finely sliced
a sprinkle of fish sauce
a garlic clove finely sliced

Shell, de-vein and remove the heads of the raw prawns, rinse well in cold water then slice very finely.

Lay on individual serving spoons or on a serving platter then top each one with a touch of bitter melon followed by a sliver of garlic.

Sprinkle with a touch of fish sauce and serve immediately.

Eat in one mouthful and enjoy. X

Keep the prawn shells and heads to make stock (see page 10).
It's very quick to do and you can freeze it even if you don't use it immediately.

Seafood

Pad Hoi Lai Nam Prik Pow - Stir Fried Mussels with Chilli Jam

2 tablespoons of garlic
2 medium red chillies - optional
a pinch of sea salt
4 tablespoons of vegetable oil
1 kilo of mussels - wash and de-beard them and discard any that remain open
3 tablespoons of chicken stock - see page 10 for instructions
2 tablespoons of chilli jam see page 66
2 tablespoons of fish sauce
a large handful of sweet basil leaves washed well and removed from the stalks

Pound the garlic and chillies in a pestle and mortar with a pinch of salt until you have a coarse paste.
Heat the oil in a wok and fry the paste until fragrant.
Add the mussels to the pan and stir with a metal spoon and as they are cooking sprinkle with the stock.
Stir in the chilli jam and fish sauce.
Finally when the mussels are open quickly stir the basil leaves through allowing them to wilt and serve in the pan if possible to maintain the heat.
Discard any mussels that have not opened during cooking.

Hoi Malaeng Phue Ob - Steamed Mussels with Nahm Jim Seafood Sauce

Dip Ingredients:
6 cloves of garlic
15 medium green chillies stems removed
a pinch of table salt
1 tablespoon of lime juice
1 tablespoon of stock or water - see page 10 for instructions
1 teaspoon of soft brown sugar
2 tablespoons of fish sauce (this is optional depending on taste)
2 tablespoons of chopped coriander leaves
Other Ingredients:
1 kilo of mussels

First prepare the dip by pounding the garlic, chillies and salt. Stir in the lime juice and a bit of water or stock and brown sugar and combine well to allow the sugar to dissolve.
Add in the fish sauce and taste and re adjust the seasoning if necessary.
Briefly stir in the coriander and pour into a serving dish.

Wash the mussels and discard any that remain open.
Steam the mussels, using the water from inside a coconut or plain water, until they open and have just cooked.
Discard any mussels that have not opened during cooking and serve immediately.

You can also make these recipes with clams and the result will be sweeter X

Steaming mussels in coconut water
is a great tip I got from Ning X

Tod Maan

Thai Fishcakes

The trick to making great aerated fishcakes is to throw the mixture into a metal bowl repeatedly from side to side X

Paste Ingredients:
10 large dried red chillies - cut into 5cm pieces soaked and de-seeded
1 1/2 tablespoon of sliced galangal
3 tablespoons of sliced lemongrass
1 tablespoon of coriander root scraped
2 teaspoons of kaffir lime zest - omit this if you can't get it
2 tablespoons of garlic
1 tablespoon of shallots
1 tablespoon of dry roasted shrimp paste
a pinch of sea salt

Other Ingredients:
300g of boneless white fish
1 batch of red curry paste
3 tablespoons of fish sauce
1 teaspoon of white sugar
1 egg lightly beaten
2 tablespoons of finely sliced snake beans
5 lime leaves, stems removed, rolled and finely shredded
vegetable oil for deep frying

First make the cucumber relish and set aside followed by the paste see page 12 for instructions.

Wash the fish in salted water and shred with a cleaver.
Put the fish in a pestle and mortar and pound then stir in the paste, fish sauce and the sugar.
Add in enough egg to make the mixture bind but not be too sloppy.

Now for the fun - throw the mixture against the side of a metal bowl again and again for a few minutes.
The mixture will become more elastic as you do this.

Finally mix in the beans and lime leaves.
Split into small balls, flatten a bit and deep fry till cooked and serve immediately with the cucumber relish.

Ajad Dtaeng Kwa - Cucumber Relish

Simply mix :
2 tablespoons of long fresh chillies ideally mixed colours cut into 1/2cm rounds
3 tablespoons of finely chopped cucumber
2 tablespoons of sliced shallots
2 tablespoons of roasted and ground peanuts
1/2 cup of water
1/2 cup of rice vinegar
3 tablespoons of sugar

You can use sea bass or even cod fillet for this recipe if you cant get catfish.
If you are using a strong smelling fish like catfish then wash it with a mixture of water and white rice vinegar then dry it well. Deep fry the fish and de-bone before using which will produce a rich and flavourful dish.
If however you are using a boneless fillet you can cut out all of this process and in this case the dish will taste lighter and fresher..

Pla Duk Pat Prik Gaeng

Catfish with Paste

Paste Ingredients:
10-15 medium red dried chillies
1/2 teaspoon of sea salt
1 tablespoon of lemongrass
1 teaspoon of galangal
2 tablespoons of shallots
1 tablespoon of garlic

Other Ingredients:
2 tablespoons of vegetable oil and oil for deep frying
a batch of paste as above
450g of catfish, sea bass or any white fish
250ml of coconut milk - see page 8 for instructions
1 cup of shredded grachai (optional) or you could use white turmeric
5 kaffir lime leaves - de veined and torn
5 young green peppercorns
2 tablespoons of fish sauce
1/2 teaspoon of white sugar (optional)
1 cup of holy basil
large red chilli cut into strips

First make the paste - see page 12 for instructions.

Fry the paste in 2 tablespoons of oil for about three minutes until it starts to smell cooked.

Add the fish and gently rotate to coat being careful not to break it up.

Add the coconut milk and bring to the boil, simmer until the fish is almost cooked through.

Add in the grachai, peppercorns and lime leaves and simmer until the vegetables are lightly cooked.

Season with the fish sauce and a little sugar (if using).

Stir in the holy basil and chilli strips, immediately remove from the heat and serve.

This lady makes fabulous fishcakes every day on Thanon Nakornchaisri in the Dusit area of Bangkok x

Hor Mok

Steamed Fish in Banana Leaves

I love to serve these at a dinner party as they look so impressive but all the work can be done beforehand and then you just put them in the steamer as the guests have their first drink.
These baskets are often stapled together but I find this hazardous so generally I pin them with wooden toothpicks..
It should be noted that they are better eaten hot but they cool quickly..

Red paste Ingredients:
10 large dried red chillies - cut into 5cm pieces soaked and de-seeded
a pinch of sea salt
1 1/2 tablespoon of sliced galangal
3 tablespoons of sliced lemongrass
1 tablespoon of coriander root scraped
2 teaspoons of kaffir lime zest - omit this if you can't get it
2 tablespoons of garlic
1 tablespoon of shallots
1 tablespoon of dry roasted shrimp paste

Other Ingredients:
enough banana leaves to make 8-12 baskets for steaming
2 tablespoons of red paste
1 3/4 cup of rich coconut cream - reduced by boiling - keep half a cup to mix with the paste and a quarter of a cup for topping - you can use canned for this or see page 8 for instructions
400g of boneless white fish fillets pounded in a pestle and mortar and drained
1 egg
1 1/2 tablespoons of fish sauce
a pinch of table salt
a handful of sweet basil leaves
5 kaffir lime leaves, stems removed, rolled together and finely shredded
a handful of coriander leaves
3 long red chillies cut into slivers

First make the paste see page 12 for instructions.
Make the banana steamer cups and set aside.
Using a wooden spatula stir the paste into the coconut cream.
Add in the pounded fish, making sure it is dry before you do this.
Break the egg into the mixture and stir briskly for a couple of minutes.
Season with the fish sauce and salt.
Place some sweet basil leaves in the bottom of each cup then divide the mixture between the banana cups.
Steam the cups for twenty minutes.
Use the rich coconut cream, lime leaves, coriander leaves and red chillies to garnish each one, allow to cool a little before serving.

Pad Cha

Fried Seafood with Grachai

Paste ingredients:
1 tablespoon of large red chillies
1 tablespoon of medium red chillies
1 tablespoon of large yellow chillies
1 tablespoon of garlic
1/2 teaspoon of sea salt

Other Ingredients:
2 tablespoons of vegetable oil
200g of raw prawns peeled, de-veined and cleaned
100g of squid scored with a criss-cross pattern and cleaned
2 teaspoons of fish sauce
1 teaspoon of oyster sauce
1 cup of finely shredded grachai
2/3rds of a cup of young green peppercorn stalks
1/2 cup of holy basil or Thai basil leaves
1 tablespoon of large red chillies cut into strips
1/4 cup of kaffir lime leaves finely shredded

Make a paste by pounding the chillies, garlic and salt then set aside.

Fry the paste in the vegetable oil for a minute.

Add the prawns and squid then stir until they are just cooked.

Add the fish sauce and oyster sauce and cook for another minute.

Quickly stir through the grachai, green peppercorn stalks and basil and fry briefly.

Pour into a serving bowl and decorate with the strips of chilli and shredded lime leaves.

Pla Nueng Manao

Steamed Sea Bass with Chilli Lime Sauce

1 kilo of Sea bass - cleaned, de-scaled and gutted but leave the head, tail and fins intact
a pinch of table salt
a pinch of ground white pepper
2 tablespoons of coriander leaves - leaves and stems chopped
10-15 birds eye chillies finely chopped
6 garlic cloves chopped
2 tablespoons of pickled garlic - outer sheaths removed and chopped
2-3 tablespoons of pickled garlic juice
4-5 tablespoons of lime juice
3 tablespoons of fish sauce
1/4 cup of chicken stock - see page 10 for instructions
1 lime sliced for garnishing
2 spring onions - use the bottom part only sliced then soak them in cold water so that they curl up
1/4 cup of Chinese celery cut into 2.5cm strips

Score the cleaned and prepared fish on both sides and pat dry.
Season with salt and pepper and put aside in a bowl that is suitable to steam it in.

In a mixing bowl mix the coriander, chopped chillies, garlic, pickled garlic, pickled garlic juice, lime juice and fish sauce. Stir well to mix and put aside.

Pour the chicken stock over the fish and place it in the steamer.
Steam for 12-17 minutes depending on the size of the fish until cooked through.

Remove it from the steamer and drizzle the sauce over the whole fish.

Garnish with the lime slices, spring onion curls and Chinese celery and serve immediately.

A simple and fresh way to steam fish X

Talay Pad Pong Khari

Stir Fried Seafood with Curry Paste

1 egg lightly whisked
1/2 tablespoon of chilli jam - see page 66 for recipe
1 teaspoon of fish sauce
1 teaspoon of light soy sauce
3 raw prawns de-veined and butterflied
12 squid sliced and scored with a criss -cross pattern
100g of cooked crab meat - you could even use good quality canned
2 cloves of garlic
2 tablespoons of vegetable oil
1 1/2 tablespoons of Chinese curry powder
1/2 cup of sliced onions
1/4 cup of coconut cream - you can use the top part of canned coconut milk or see page 8 for instructions
1/4 cup of fish stock - see page 10 for instructions
1/1/2 teaspoons of sugar
2 spring onions sliced
1 tablespoon of coriander leaves
2 large red chillies sliced crossways

In a mixing bowl combine the lightly beaten egg with the chilli jam, fish sauce, soy sauce, prawns and squid. If the crab is cooked then do not add it at this stage, however if it is uncooked put it in too.

Fry the garlic in the oil for a minute then add the curry powder and fry until the paste starts to smell cooked.

Add the onions and the fish/egg mixture to the pan and cook stirring constantly.

Quickly add the coconut cream and season with fish stock and sugar.

If you are using cooked crab add it now.

When cooked, stir in the spring onion and coriander leaves and serve immediately garnished with the red chillies.

Because this dish is best made over a high temperature gas burner you need to get everything ready to go and cook this dish as fast as possible for best results.

Pla Tod Sauce Mamuang

Sea Bass Fillets with Green Mango

4 pieces of sea bass fillet (or any white fish)
a large pinch of table salt
vegetable oil for deep frying
8 tablespoons of shredded green mango

Dressing Ingredients:
4 tablespoons of fish sauce
4 tablespoons of lime juice or to taste
2 teaspoon of caster sugar or to taste
10-12 finely sliced chillies
4 tablespoons garlic finely sliced

Marinate the fish with a large pinch of salt for a couple of hours before cooking.
First deep-fry the fish and then, if necessary, de-bone with tongs and remove the skin.
Put the fillets on one side whilst you make the sauce.
Make up the sauce by mixing the fish sauce and half of the lime juice, add sugar to taste.
Chop the chillies and garlic and mix then balance the taste with the remaining lime juice.
The final balance is up to you, it depends how you like it.
Deep fry the fish again until golden brown and serve with the mango on one side and the dipping sauce in a bowl. When you eat it combine it all together to taste on your plate.

Pla Rad Prik Sam Sod

Deep Fried Fish with Three Flavoured Sauce

2 tablespoons sliced long red chillies
2 tablespoons of red bell pepper
a pinch of sea salt
2 tablespoons of coriander root scraped
2 tablespoons of garlic
2 tablespoons of vegetable oil
1 tablespoon of rice vinegar
1 1/2 tablespoons of sugar
1 1/2 tablespoons of tangerine juice
1 1/2 tablespoons of fish sauce
1/2 teaspoon of tapioca flour
1 whole sea bass de-scaled
vegetable oil for deep frying plus 2 tablespoons

Pound the chillies and red pepper with a pinch of salt and set aside.

Next pound the coriander root and garlic in a pestle and mortar and set aside.

Fry the coriander and garlic paste for a minute in two tablespoons of oil then add the chilli paste and fry for another two minutes.

Gradually season the sauce with the rice vinegar, sugar, tangerine juice, and fish sauce.
Adjust to taste - if the tangerine is sour use less vinegar. If necessary add another touch of salt.

Coat the fish in tapioca flour and deep fry.

Gently reheat the sauce and cover the fish with it before serving.

Garnish with coriander leaves to serve.

This makes an impressive centrepiece to a meal but it's actually really simple to make.

Such a classic Thai sweet and sour taste X

Hurrah for Magic paste!

Pla Muk Yad Sai

Squid Stuffed with Pork and Prawns

150g of pork - choose some with about 15% fat
8 raw prawns washed, peeled and de-veined
a pinch of table salt
400g of cleaned squid
5 coriander roots scraped
10 whole white peppercorns
2 cloves of garlic
1 teaspoon of cornflour
1 tablespoon light soy sauce
white only from 1/2 egg

With a heavy cleaver combine and mince the pork and prawn chopping it repeatedly until you have a finely cut, well combined mince adding a pinch of salt as you go. It also works well to slide your cleaver through a garlic clove a few times whilst you are doing this.

In a pestle and mortar make a paste from the coriander roots, white pepper and garlic adding a pinch of salt.

Mix the paste with the meat and prawn mixture and add the cornflour and soy sauce.

Put to one side to marinate for thirty minutes.

After marinating gradually add in the egg white using as much as you need to get a firm consistency but do not make the mixture too runny.

Prepare the squid by removing the tentacles with a gentle pulling motion.
Keep these to one side as you are going to use them later. Reach just inside the squid and gently remove the long quill - make sure you get it all as sometimes these break in half. Slice off the the wings but keep them to use in a soup later. Stuff each squid with the mixture and steam until cooked along with the reserved tentacles. This should take about 15 minutes.

For a delicious alternative to these steamed stuffed squid allow them to cool and then shallow fry turning frequently, until golden, slice and serve with deep fried chopped garlic on top.

Serve the steamed squid with the following dip:

3 tablespoons of fish sauce
3 tablespoons of lime juice
2 chopped chillies
2 shallots sliced
1/2 sliced lime cut into small squares

Yam Pla Duk Fuu

Puffy Catfish Salad

2 whole catfish BBQ'd or grilled until cooked - you can also buy these ready cooked in oriental shops
vegetable oil for deep frying

Dip Ingredients:
5-7 birds eye chillies
2 coriander roots scraped
1 teaspoon of table salt
3 tablespoons of lime juice
1-2 teaspoons of caster sugar
2-3 tablespoons of fish sauce
2 tablespoons of lemongrass (optional)

Salad Ingredients:
1/2 shredded green mango
1 cup of chopped mint
1/2 cup of Chinese celery chopped into 5cm pieces
1/2 cup of sliced shallots
lettuce to serve
1/4 cup of deep fried peanuts or cashew nuts

BBQ or grill the catfish then remove the skin and shred the flesh making sure that you do not include any bones.

Next make the dip by pounding the chillies and coriander root with the salt in a pestle and mortar. Add the lime juice, sugar and fish sauce. Sometimes Mae also put some finely sliced lemongrass in this dip but this is optional. As all of these items always vary in strength of flavour do everything cautiously. Add all of the lime juice then gradually add the other ingredients and balance and judge the taste as you blend. Put this dip in a small serving bowl.

To make the salad mix the mango, mint, celery and shallots and put to one side.

Heat the oil until it is really hot and smoking and deep fry the fish - it should puff up immediately and clump together. Fry for a minute then turn and cook until golden brown. You will probably have to do this in two batches. Drain on kitchen towel.

Place the fish on a bed of lettuce, cover with the salad mix and sprinkle with nuts.

Drizzle some of the dressing on the top and serve the rest on one side so that guests can adjust and mix the seasoning and salad themselves on their plates.

Carole's Tip:
Look out for really firm smooth skinned mangoes when you are shopping - they are the best!

BBQ

Khao Neow Moo Yang

Grilled Pork with Sticky Rice

5 white peppercorns
1 coriander root scraped
1 tablespoon of finely chopped garlic
a pinch of sea salt
1 tablespoon of light soy sauce
200g of pork
500g of sticky rice washed and soaked for 6 hours
1/2 cup of coconut cream - see page 8 for instructions or use canned
a selection of crunchy raw vegetables to serve

Pound the peppercorns in a pestle and mortar then add the coriander root, garlic and salt and pound together until a rough paste is made.

Stir in the soy sauce then add the pork and leave to marinate for thirty minutes.

In the meantime, drain and rinse the rice and steam for approximately thirty minutes until cooked.

Remove the pork from the marinade, brush with the coconut cream and BBQ or grill until cooked.
Allow it to cool before slicing it diagonally.

Serve with some crunchy raw vegetables, slices of lime and Esarn Jaew dip.

Esarn Jaew - Esarn Chilli Dip

This is great with grilled meats. Just mix all the ingredients, taste and adjust to taste.

1 tablespoon of chilli flakes
1 tablespoon of lime juice
1/2 tablespoon of tamarind paste
3 tablespoons of fish sauce
1 teaspoon of caster sugar
1 tablespoon of finely sliced spring onion
1 teaspoon of coriander leaves to decorate
sprinkle with a little dry fried rice (optional)

The best Thai charcoal is made
from 100% chemical free
Mangrove wood which burns
slowly at high temperatures ...

Tom Kloang

Fish and Vegetable Soup

This recipe is a repeat from the soup section but I particularly wanted to draw your attention to it when your mind is on the BBQ x

BBQ the following ingredients and put on one side to cool and when cooled discard the skins
1 tablespoon of galangal
1 tablespoon of lemongrass
1 tablespoon of garlic cloves whole with the skin on
1 tablespoon of shallots whole with the skin on
1 cup of white fish

Other Ingredients:
500ml of water
1/2 cup mushrooms sliced
1 tablespoon of fish sauce
3 kaffir lime leaves
5 medium green fresh chillies
1 tablespoon of coriander leaves
1 tablespoon of spring onions chopped into 5cm pieces
1 tablespoon of chopped sawtooth coriander
1 tablespoon of lime juice
5 large dried chillies deep fried for decoration

First prepare and BBQ all the ingredients as above list, allow them to cool and when cooled discard the skins.

In a small pan bring the water to a boil and add the mushrooms, galangal and lemongrass.
Add the fish and season with fish sauce.

Add the BBQ'd garlic and shallots to the pan.

Bruise the chillies with a pestle and mortar and add to the soup.

Reduce the heat and add the chopped coriander, spring onion and sawtoothed coriander.
Finally put the lime juice in the shared serving bowl and ladle the soup into that.

Garnish with the deep fried chillies and serve immediately.

This great BBQ attachment protects the meat from direct heat and creates a delicious sauce in the rim

Sue Rong Hai

Crying Beef

"rong hai" means crying and so this BBQ dish is most commonly known as crying beef because juices fall like tears from it as it slowly roasts on the grill.

Marinade Ingredients:
2 coriander roots scraped
a pinch of sea salt
1 tablespoon of light soy sauce
1 tablespoon of oyster sauce
a pinch of caster sugar
400g of steak - a grainy steak works best for this dish

Dressing Ingredients:
4-5 tablespoons of fish sauce
4 tablespoons of lime juice
a pinch of caster sugar
1/2 tablespoon of chilli flakes
2 tablespoons of dry fried ground rice
1 tablespoon of chopped spring onions

To Serve:
1/2 cucumber cut into strips
2 finely sliced tomatoes
2 limes quartered

Pound the coriander root with a pinch of salt in a pestle and mortar to make a paste then mix in the soy and oyster sauces and stir in the sugar.

Marinate the beef in this mixture for twenty minutes then BBQ or grill until rare or medium rare depending on how you like it.

Whilst the meat is resting make up the dressing by mixing the fish sauce, lime juice, sugar, chilli flakes, dry fried ground rice and chopped spring onions.

Slice the beef finely on the diagonal and splay out on a serving dish then pour the dressing over the steak or, if you prefer, serve it on the side as a dipping sauce.

Eat with finely sliced cucumber, tomatoes and lime quarters.

Yam Nue

Barbecued Beef Salad

3 coriander roots scraped
a pinch of sea salt
1 tablespoon of light soy sauce to marinate
1 tablespoon of oyster sauce to marinate
a pinch of caster sugar to marinate
400g of steak - a grainy cut works best for this

Dip Ingredients:
a pinch of table salt
2 tablespoons of garlic pounded in a pestle and mortar
2 tablespoons of medium red chillies pounded in a pestle and mortar
5-6 tablespoons of chicken stock - see page 10 for instructions
4 tablespoons of fish sauce
4 tablespoons of lime juice
1 tablespoon of palm sugar - if it is not soft heat it briefly in the microwave
2 tablespoons of sliced shallots
4 tablespoons of shredded green mango - or you can use sliced green aubergine or a mixture of the two
2 tablespoons of kaffir lime leaves stems removed and finely shredded
2 tablespoons of lemongrass very finely sliced on the diagonal

Salad Ingredients:
a handful of raw vegetables such as cucumber, Thai aubergines, lettuce and chillies

First make the dipping sauce by mixing all the ingredients together and put on one side.

Pound the coriander root in a pestle and mortar with a pinch of salt and mix with the soy sauce, oyster sauce and the sugar.

Marinate the beef in this mixture for twenty minutes then BBQ or grill until rare to medium rare then put it on one side and allow to rest.

Slice the steak on the diagonal and lay on a serving platter.

Serve with the raw vegetable salad and the dipping sauce.

This recipe really is at its best if you can barbecue the beef but you will still get a reasonable result if you grill it.

Simply pop a banana on the embers to make a scrummy little dessert X

Preaw Wan

Sweet and Sour Sauce

This is the sauce served on Thai street stalls with Gai Yang chicken but it works well with any grilled meat so it's a useful recipe.

1 tablespoon of long red chillies
1 teaspoon of medium red chillies
1 tablespoon of garlic
2 teaspoons of sea salt
1 cup of water
3/4 cup of white rice vinegar
3/4 cup of sugar

In a pestle and mortar pound the two types of chillies, garlic and salt and set aside.
Bring the water and vinegar to the boil then add the sugar and allow it to dissolve fully and thicken slightly.
The liquid will have reduced by about half by the time this happens.
Reduce the heat and add in the paste.
Season with another pinch of table salt to sharpen the taste.

Put into a serving dish and allow to cool before serving.

Dips

Nahm Prik Gapi

Shrimp Paste Dipping Sauce

The importance of this dish to Thai food cannot be underestimated. This was something that was eaten everyday in the olden days, it was a real staff of life. Nowadays it has fallen out of favour and although you see a lot of Nahm Prik Gapi and steamed mackerel in the mornings on the streets of Bangkok it tends to be the older residents that are drawn to it.
You can usually find these steamed mackerel sold in their baskets in the freezer in Thai supermarkets which means you can deep fry them straight from frozen to accompany this dip. It should also be served with steamed rice and raw vegetables.

I must explain that often the UK we consider that the focal point of a meal is the meat dish and all else supports it.
However in Thailand rice is the focal point and all other items just add flavour to the rice and this is very much the case with this dish. Do not expect to eat a large volume as this is a strong and some would say acquired taste!

3/4 teaspoon of shrimp paste dry fried or roasted
1 tablespoon of peeled garlic
1-2 tablespoons of dried shrimp pounded in a pestle and mortar to a fine powder
1 teaspoon of birds eye chillies
1 teaspoon of round green aubergine
3 pea aubergines removed from the stems and bruised
2 tablespoons of lime juice
1 tablespoon of fish sauce
1 teaspoon of palm sugar
1-2 whole steamed mackerel - you can buy these frozen in oriental stores they come in little open weave baskets
a handful of fresh vegetables of your choice such as cucumber, eggplant and cabbage to eat raw
a handful of lightly steamed vegetables of your choice such as string beans, wing beans and aubergines

Pound the shrimp paste with the garlic and when fully blended add the previously pounded dried shrimp, chillies and both types of aubergines and pound well.

Stir the paste well then stir in the lime juice, fish sauce and palm sugar.

Put into a serving bowl and set aside.

Prepare a platter with the fresh vegetables and lightly steam the other vegetables.
The steamed vegetables do not need to be served hot so don't worry about them cooling.

Deep fry the fish, add to the platter and serve with steamed jasmine rice.

Nahm Jim Towjaew

Fermented Soybean Dip

This dip works really well with all seafood but in particular it's great with steamed fish and boiled rice.

Mash 4 tablespoons of fermented soybeans in a pestle and mortar and stir in the following-

1 tablespoon of finely sliced chillies
1 tablespoon of coriander leaves and stems
1 tablespoon of finely chopped garlic
1 tablespoon of finely chopped ginger
1 teaspoon of caster sugar
1 tablespoon of light soy sauce
2-3 tablespoons of lime juice

When you have finished mixing the ingredients taste and adjust them.
The dip should be both salty and sour.

Prik Nahm Pla

Salty Chilli Dip

This is an everyday dip, simple and quick to put together and it should always be on the table with a Thai meal.

5 sliced green birds eye chillies
5 sliced medium red chillies
2 cloves of garlic cut into rounds
3 tablespoons of fish sauce
2 tablespoons of lime juice

Use more or less lime according to strength but the flavour of the lime and fish sauce should be equally balanced.

Esarn Jaew

Esarn Chilli Dip

This is great with grilled meats.
Just mix all the ingredients, stir well and adjust to taste.

1 tablespoon of chilli flakes
1 teaspoon of caster sugar
1 tablespoon of finely sliced spring onion
1 tablespoon of lime juice
1/2 tablespoon of tamarind paste
3 tablespoons of fish sauce
1 teaspoon of coriander leaves to garnish
Sprinkle with a little dry fried rice (optional)

Don't forget to also put extra fish sauce, sugar and chilli flakes on the table..........

Lon Goong

Prawn and Coconut Dip

Serve this dip at room temperature along with crunchy raw string beans, cucumber, chunks of cabbage and white turmeric.

1 tablespoon of chopped shallots
1 tablespoon of scraped and chopped coriander root
a pinch of table salt
100g of coarsely minced pork
150g of raw prawns
1 cup of freshly made coconut milk see page 8 for instructions
1 1/2 tablespoons of fish sauce
1 tablespoon of palm sugar - soften in the microwave if necessary
1 tablespoon of thick tamarind juice
1 tablespoon finely sliced chillies
2 tablespoons finely sliced shallots

Garnish Ingredients:
1 tablespoon of sliced medium chillies
1 tablespoon of chopped coriander leaves

In a pestle and mortar pound the shallots and coriander root with a pinch of table salt to make a paste.

With a cleaver make the pork and prawns into a mince and combine together then massage the paste into the meat and prawn mixture.

Heat the coconut milk in a pan and bring it to the boil stirring constantly to prevent the oil from separating. After a couple of minutes add the pork and prawns to the coconut milk and stir well to ensure the pieces break up.

After a few minutes add the fish sauce, softened palm sugar and tamarind juice.
Stir well then add the chillies and shallots.

Remove from the heat and put into a serving bowl and garnish with pieces of chilli and coriander.
Allow to cool before eating and serve at room temperature but don't refrigerate otherwise it will solidify.

Prik Nahm Pla
Prik Nahm Som
LON GOONG
ESARN JAEW

Nahm Jim Towjaew
Ajad Dtaeng Kwa
Nahm Jim Talay

Prik Nahm Som - Chillies in Vinegar

This is an everyday dip that is always served with noodles but actually it's just great to spice up almost anything. Slice long red or yellow chillies and cover them with rice wine vinegar.

Nahm Jim Talay - Seafood Dip

6 cloves of garlic
15 medium green chillies stems removed
a pinch of table salt
1 tablespoon of lime juice
1 tablespoon of stock or water
1 teaspoon of soft brown sugar
2 tablespoons of fish sauce (this is optional depending on taste)
2 tablespoons of chopped coriander leaves

Prepare the dip by pounding the garlic, chillies and salt.
Stir in the lime juice, a bit of water or stock, and the brown sugar and combine well to allow the sugar to dissolve.
Add in the fish sauce and taste and balance if necessary.
Briefly stir in the coriander and pour into a serving dish.

Ajad Dtaeng Kwa - Cucumber Relish

Simply mix the following and stir well then sprinkle the ground peanuts on top if you are using them.

2 tablespoons of long fresh chillies ideally mixed colours cut into 1/2cm rounds
3 tablespoons of finely chopped cucumber
2 tablespoons of sliced shallots
1/2 a cup water
1/2 a cup rice vinegar
3 tablespoons of caster sugar
2 tablespoons of roasted and ground peanuts (optional)

Kai Tod Cha-Om

Acacia Omelette

6 eggs

1 tablespoon of fish sauce

2 tablespoons of light soy sauce

3-4 handfuls of acacia leaves

3 tablespoons of vegetable oil

Break the eggs into a bowl and whisk then stir in all the other ingredients.

Heat the oil and fry the mixture in a frying pan slowly until firmly set.

Be patient because if not the outside will be burnt before it is cooked inside.

Test the middle part with a wooden skewer to ensure it has properly cooked through before serving.

Nibbles and Canapés

Talay Nueng

Seafood Canapé

I often serve this recipe on individual oriental spoons when people arrive for dinner at my supper clubs because it looks pretty and as it's served at room temperature it takes the pressure off cooking something at the last minute. Carole X

Dip Ingredients:
1 coriander root scraped
3 garlic cloves
2 whole birds eye chillies with the ends removed
a pinch of kaffir lime zest - omit this if you can't get it see page 19 for more details
1 teaspoon of kaffir lime juice - omit this if you can't get it see page 19 for more details
5 tablespoons of lime juice
5 tablespoons of fish sauce
1/2 teaspoon of caster sugar

Salad Ingredients:
200g of mixed seafood
mixed lettuce leaves
1 tablespoon of shallots finely chopped
1 tablespoon of lime leaves de-veined and finely shredded
1 tablespoon of finely sliced ginger
1 tablespoon of finely sliced chillies
1 tablespoon of finely sliced lemongrass
1 tablespoon of chopped coriander leaves
1 tablespoon of chopped mint

First make the dip. In a pestle and mortar pound the coriander root, garlic, chilli and kaffir lime zest until well blended. Add the kaffir lime juice, lime juice, fish sauce and sugar and stir well.

To make the salad, steam or sear the seafood and put to one side. Chop into small pieces if necessary.

Break up the lettuce leaves and split between the serving spoons if you are serving it this way or lay out on a platter if you are serving on a plate.

Arrange the seafood on top of the leaves and top with a pinch of all the remaining ingredients: shallots, lime leaves, ginger, chillies, lemongrass, coriander and mint.

Pour a little of the dressing over the seafood and serve.

Peek Gai Yad Sai

Stuffed Chicken Wings

This recipe really showcases the use of coriander root.
Nowadays people often eat this dipped in tempura batter before deep frying but Mae preferred the traditional way.

500g of chicken wings - skinned and de-boned
2 tablespoons of fish sauce
2 tablespoons of light soy sauce
vegetable oil for deep frying

Stuffing Ingredients:
50g of pork
50g of raw prawns
10 white peppercorns
1 coriander root scraped
a pinch of table salt
4 cloves of garlic

Marinate the chicken wings with the fish sauce and soy sauce for an hour.
Chop the pork and prawn mixture with a cleaver and blend together.
Pound the white peppercorns in a pestle and mortar then add in the coriander root and salt and pound again then finally pound in the garlic.
When blended add in the pork and prawn mixture and stir well then put aside.
With your fingers gently create a pocket in the side of the chicken wings and fill with the stuffing.
Shallow fry the wings slowly until browned, this will prevent the stuffing from coming out when you deep fry them.
Deep fry until golden, drain well to prevent them being oily and serve with sweet and sour chilli sauce.

Dip Ingredients:
2.5cm of long red chillies
1 teaspoon of medium red chillies
1 tablespoon of garlic
2 teaspoons of salt
1 cup of water
3/4 cup of white rice vinegar
3/4 cup of sugar
a pinch of salt

In a pestle and mortar pound the two types of chillies, garlic and salt and set aside.
Bring the water and vinegar to the boil then add the sugar and allow it to dissolve fully and thicken slightly.
The liquid will have reduced by about half by the time this happens.
Reduce the heat and add in the paste.
Season with another pinch of salt to sharpen the taste.
Put into a serving dish and allow to cool before serving.

Poh Plah Muu

Steamed Pork in Rice Pancakes

1/2 cup of light soy sauce
1/2 cup of dark soy sauce
300g of pork - you can use any cut but you don't want too much fat in it
3 carrots
a pinch of table salt
edible flowers
lettuce - choose decorative types with colour in mind
6 rice pancakes

First make the dip listed below as it takes quite a while to cool.

Mix the two soy sauces together and marinate the pork in it for at least thirty minutes then drain and steam the pork until it is cooked.

Cut the carrots into long strips with a potato peeler and quickly blanch in boiling water with a pinch of salt then plunge them into cold iced water to retain their colour.
Wash the flowers in white vinegar and wash the lettuce in water.

Lay the pancakes between a clean wet tea towel that has been rung out, until they soften.
Alternatively you could dip them in water but I prefer the drier result you get with the tea towel method.

Lay the pancakes out, place all the ingredients inside them decoratively and fold up the bottom then roll them up tightly.

Dipping Sauce Ingredients:
1 tablespoon of long red chillies
1 teaspoon of medium red chillies
1 tablespoon of garlic
2 teaspoons of sea salt
1 cup of water
3/4 cup of white rice vinegar
3/4 cup of sugar

In a pestle and mortar pound the two types of chillies, garlic and salt and set aside.
Bring the water and vinegar to the boil then add the sugar and allow it to dissolve fully and thicken slightly. The liquid will have reduced by about half by the time this happens.
Reduce the heat and add in the paste.
Season with another pinch of table salt to sharpen the taste.
Put into a serving dish and allow to cool before serving.

I have had great success making this with rib of beef, leftover from a Sunday lunch, which I combined with asparagus spears.

Borage would make an attractive alternative to the purple flowers but any edible flowers will work and help you to create your own style.

Muu Gratium Prik Thai

Deep Fried Pork Cakes

400g of pork with about 10% fat
12 raw prawns peeled and de-veined
a pinch of table salt
5 white peppercorns
2 coriander roots scraped and chopped
1 whole clove of garlic
a pinch of sea salt
1 tablespoon of light soy sauce
1 tablespoon of fish sauce
vegetable oil for deep frying
4 tablespoons of finely chopped garlic for topping
a sprinkle of ground white pepper

Pound the pork and prawns together with a cleaver to make a mince, adding a pinch of table salt in the process.

Pound the white peppercorns in a pestle and mortar then add in the coriander root, garlic and sea salt then pound again.

Add in the pork and prawn mixture, season with the soy and fish sauce, stir well and set aside for thirty minutes.

Meantime deep fry the chopped garlic until it is golden and reserve for the topping.

Form the cakes into flattened balls and deep fry until brown.

Lay on a serving platter and decorate with the fried garlic and a sprinkle of ground white pepper.

Kao Tod Nam Sod

Pickled Pork with Deep Fried Rice

This is a great way to use up cooked rice.. These two dishes are meant to be cooked together, as after they are made they are combined to make one dish.
However, you can make the rice balls alone to eat with other things and often I make mini versions to serve as canapé. x

Red Curry Paste Ingredients:
10 large dried red chillies - cut into 5cm pieces soaked and de-seeded
a pinch of sea salt
1 1/2 tablespoon of sliced galangal
3 tablespoons of sliced lemongrass
1 tablespoon of coriander root scraped
2 teaspoons of kaffir lime zest - omit this if you can't get it
2 tablespoons of garlic
1 tablespoon of shallots
1 tablespoon of dry roasted shrimp paste

Rice Ball Ingredients:
2 cups of iced soda water
1/2 tablespoon of rice flour
2 cups of cooked jasmine rice
1 tablespoon of red curry paste
1 tablespoon of fish sauce
2 teaspoons of palm sugar - softened
1/2 egg lightly whisked

Picked Pork Ingredients:
2 cups of pork belly with 20% fat
a pinch of salt
2 tablespoons of minced garlic
1 tablespoon of fish sauce
1 teaspoon of dried chilli powder
1 tablespoon of ground sticky rice
juice of 1 lime
2 spring onions sliced
2 shredded lime leaves to decorate

Salad Ingredients:
1/4 cup of shredded young ginger
1/2 cup of deep fried peanuts
1/2 tablespoon of medium green chillies sliced diagonally
2 tablespoons of shallots
1 lettuce
2 large red chillies - deep fried for topping
a handful of washed coriander - to serve

First make the red curry paste - see page 12 for instructions.

To make the rice balls:
Put the iced soda water in a bowl and mix in the rice flour and put to one side.
Mix the remaining ingredients together thoroughly. Make sure that you judge how much egg to add as you do not want the mixture to be too sloppy.
Roll into balls and dip each one in the flour mixture and deep fry until yellow.

To make the pickled pork:
Remove the skin from the pork and boil until it is opaque and cooked through skimming occasionally then drain. Allow it to cool and chop into very small strips. Please note that the use of the pork skin in this dish is optional.
Mince the remaining pork and massage the salt into it along with the minced garlic for about twenty minutes until it starts to smell sour then set aside for thirty minutes. Dry fry the pork mixture.
Crumble the cooked rice balls and mix together with the pickled pork and pork skin if using.
Do this gently as you do not want the rice balls to break up completely.
Season with fish sauce, chilli powder, ground sticky rice and lime juice.
Break up one of the deep fried chillies and mix in but reserve one to use as garnish.
Finally mix in the spring onion. Top with the shredded lime leaves.

Mix the salad from the listed ingredients and serve with the coriander leaves on the side.

Nuea Sawarn

Heavenly Beef

1 tablespoon of black peppercorns
2 tablespoons of coriander seeds - dry fried
4 big cloves of garlic
500g of rump steak finely sliced across the grain
3 tablespoons of caster sugar
4 tablespoons of fish sauce
vegetable oil for deep frying
2 tablespoons of chopped coriander leaves

In a pestle and mortar grind the black pepper and coriander seeds before pounding in the garlic.
Massage the beef into the mixture and then add in the sugar and fish sauce.
Lay on a wire rack on top of a baking tray to allow the juices to drip and bake in an oven at 50c for about an hour or until dry. This is to replicate sun drying which is rarely possible in Britain!
Allow to cool and then deep fry until golden brown.
You can eat these hot but I think they are at their best at room temperature scattered with the coriander leaves.

Gai Hor Bai Toey

Chicken in Pandanus

These are quite simple to make and wrap. If you are having any trouble securing the leaves use a toothpick to secure the ends as it's much easier, still looks pretty and gives your guests something to eat with.

5 white peppercorns
2 coriander roots scraped
1/2 tablespoon of garlic cloves
1 teaspoon of sea salt
1 tablespoon of light soy sauce
1 teaspoon of black soy sauce
2 1/2 tablespoons of roasted sesame seeds
500g of chicken cut into 2.5 cm cubes
a big bunch of pandanus leaves
vegetable oil for deep frying
black vinegar to use as a dip

First make a paste in a pestle and mortar out of the peppercorns, coriander root, garlic and salt.
Add the light soy sauce, black soy sauce and sesame seeds to the paste and marinate the chicken in this for a few hours or ideally overnight. However reserve some of the sesame seeds as topping.Wrap the chicken in the pandanus leaves - start by forming a cone as seen on the left then cross the longest leaf over the meat which folds the top leaf in two. Continue to wrap the leaf around another time before securing it by tucking the end in on itself or pinning with a toothpick.

Deep fry the parcels in hot oil -once the colour of the pandanus leaves leaves turns dark with a yellow hue and seems quite dry then remove them as they are ready.

Serve with a side bowl of black vinegar with some sesame seeds sprinkled on top.

Miang Kham

Betel Leaf Chewing Paste

Paste Ingredients:
1/2 cup of dried shrimp (wash well)
1/2 cup of shallots peeled and finely diced
1/2 cup of young ginger peeled and finely sliced
1/2 cup of lime - leave the peel on and finely dice
1 cup of grated and roasted coconut
1 cup of roasted or deep fried peanuts
1 tablespoon of red chillies sliced

Other Ingredients to serve:
a handful of betel leaves - wash well
deep fried peanuts
limes cut into small chunks skin on
deep fried dried shrimps
chopped shallots
grated roasted coconut
fresh whole chillies - optional

Sauce Ingredients:
1/4 cup shallots BBQ'd in their skins then peeled and sliced
1 teaspoon of galangal peeled and BBQ'd then sliced
1 cup of roasted and grated coconut
1/4 cup of peanuts roasted or deep fried, cooled then ground in a pestle and mortar
1/4 cup of dried shrimp pounded in a pestle and mortar
2 cups of water
1 1/2 cups of palm sugar
1 1/2 teaspoons of table salt
2 teaspoons of dry roasted shrimp paste

First make the paste by pounding all the ingredients one by one, the hardest ingredients first, until you form a paste.

BBQ the shallots and galangal then put them to one side. Roast or dry fry the grated coconut, deep fry the peanuts. and pound the dried shrimp.

In a pestle and mortar pound the shallots, galangal, grated coconut, dried shrimp and shrimp paste.

Mix the water and sugar together and heat in a small pan on a low heat and when it comes to the boil add the paste mixture. Mix well and add in the salt.

Simmer until it becomes sticky then add in the ground peanuts.

Put into a serving bowl and allow to cool.

Arrange a serving plate with the betel leaves on and then place all the other ingredients in separate bowls.

Taking one leaf at a time put a pinch of each ingredient in the leaf (to personal taste) and top with a little of the sauce. Wrap up the leaf. Eat the entire leaf in one bite but chew well before swallowing.

Miang Kham is like all the flavours of Thailand in one bite and it's addictive! Mae did this stylish display but I usually put all the ingredients in separate bowls, lay out the leaves and let the guests help themselves to their personal taste. Alternatively you can pre wrap them and put several on skewers so that they can be eaten without the fiddling about.

Siklong Moo Tod Kratiem Prik Thai

Spare Ribs

500g of pork ribs chopped into 5cm pieces - these ribs must be on the bone
5 white peppercorns
2 cloves of garlic
5 coriander roots scraped - 2 for the marinade and 3 for later
1 teaspoon of ground cinnamon
1/2 teaspoon white sugar
2 tablespoons of light soy sauce
1/2 teaspoon of Maggi seasoning
1 tablespoon of cornflour
oil for deep frying
4 cloves of garlic chopped and deep fried to use as topping
ground white pepper

Place the ribs in cold water and bring to the boil. Boil for 15 minutes skimming off any impurities that rise to the top.

Make a paste from the peppercorns, garlic and two of the five coriander roots. Add the cinnamon powder and stir well.

Place the ribs in the marinade and mix well, leave to marinate for thirty minutes minimum then boil again for twenty minutes.

I sometimes leave them overnight at this stage so that I can come back from work and finish them quickly.

Pound the remaining three coriander roots then add the sugar, light soy and Maggi seasoning.

Make a paste from the cornflour and a tablespoon of water and add this to the mixture.

Coat the pork ribs in the mixture and deep fry until golden brown.

Serve with lots of chopped deep fried garlic and ground white pepper as a topping.

Sai Aur

Chiangmai Sausage

Before you make these see my notes about sausage stuffing on page 155 X

Paste Ingredients:
5 tablespoons of long dried chillies cut into 2 inch pieces soaked and de-seeded
a pinch of sea salt
1 teaspoon of sliced galangal
1 tablespoon of finely sliced lemongrass
1 coriander root
a pinch of kaffir lime zest - optional
1 tablespoon of garlic
1 tablespoon of shallots
1 teaspoon of shrimp paste
1 teaspoon of chilli flakes - you should ideally use northern chilli flakes to get a smoky effect
1 tablespoon of chopped turmeric

Other Ingredients:
2 cups of pork with about 20% fat - sprinkle with a pinch of salt and finely mince with a cleaver
2 tablespoons of of Chiang Mai paste
1 tablespoon of very finely sliced lemongrass
a pinch of chilli powder
2 tablespoons of fish sauce
1/2 metre of natural intestine

First make the paste see page 12 for instructions.

Please note that because I can't get kaffir limes to zest in the UK I sometimes replace it's effect by putting two finely sliced lime leaves in the sausage mix not the paste - but this is my take on it not Mae's.

Mix the chopped pork with the paste, lemongrass and chilli powder. Season with some of the fish sauce. Deep fry a small ball of the mixture and taste and adjust accordingly - use more fish sauce or paste if you need to. When you are satisfied with the flavour, stuff and make up the sausages.
With a wooden skewer make several holes in the skin of each sausage.

Grill slowly on the low embers of a BBQ and make more holes with the wooden skewers whilst they are cooking to prevent the sausage skin splitting. If you cannot barbecue then deep fry them at medium temperature putting more holes in with a wooden skewer as they cook.

When cooked allow to cool a bit, slice and serve with sticky rice and crunchy raw vegetables.

Sai Aur served in the fabulous and organic Daradalay cafe alluringly hidden behind a garage on Phi Chai Road in Dusit

Sai Grog Esarn

Sour Esarn Sausage

1 kilo of pork with 20% fat
5 white peppercorns
3/4 cup of garlic minced or pounded in a pestle and mortar
2-3 tablespoons of table salt
1 cup of cooked sticky rice
fish sauce - optional
palm sugar - optional
1 metre of natural intestine
oil for deep frying
a handful of roasted peanuts
a few slices of peeled ginger

Chop the meat into fine mince by hand with a cleaver and put to one side.

Pound the peppercorns in a pestle and mortar until ground then add in the garlic and pound again until very smooth.

Massage the minced pork with the garlic mixture and salt for twenty minutes. It will start to smell sourer as you do this then put the mixture on one side for twenty minutes.

Combine the mixture together thoroughly with the cooked rice.

Break off a small piece and fry to taste and add a little fish sauce and sugar to the mixture if you feel it is necessary.

When you are satisfied with the taste, stuff the intestines to make the sausages just 4-5cm long and knot off. Prick in a few places with a wooden skewer.

Grill or deep fry on a medium temperature and prick more holes in as you do this to prevent splitting.

These sausages will keep for a couple of days in the fridge.

Serve with roasted peanuts and slices of fresh ginger.

Carole's Tips to making top sausages ...

It's become more difficult to buy natural sausage skin but what you need to do is find a butchers who make their own sausages and they should be able to sell you some.

If I am making a small batch I struggle along with a sausage making attachment on my food processor. It works well but it is hard work, so if I am making a big batch I make up the filling and get my local butcher to stuff them in his industrial machine.

If you buy the intestine yourself make sure that you keep it wet as it dries out and becomes brittle really quickly. Also make sure you chop the lemongrass really finely otherwise it will tend to break the skin and the sausages will taste woody.

In Thailand pink is considered to be a lucky colour on Tuesday!

Ton Jued Galamplee Yadsai

Whole Steamed Cabbage with Pork and Prawns

A whole cabbage
300g of pork with about 10% fat content
200g of raw prawns
5 white peppercorns
3 cloves of chopped garlic
3 coriander roots scraped
a pinch of sea salt
2 tablespoons of fish sauce
vegetable oil for deep frying
1/4 cup of chopped and deep fried garlic for garnish
coriander leaves

With a heavy cleaver combine and mince the pork and prawn and chop repeatedly until you have a finely combined mince. It is good to slide your cleaver through a garlic clove a few times whilst you are doing this.
Make a paste from the peppercorns, garlic, coriander root and salt.
Massage in the pork and prawn mixture and season with fish sauce.
Carefully cut a hole in the cabbage and reserve the rounds ready for the second recipe if using.
Stuff the cabbage with the mixture and steam until cooked through.
Serve immediately with some coriander leaves and fried garlic to garnish.

Make a canapé version!

You would also need: 1/2 cup of tapioca flour, 200ml of chicken stock and the yolk of an egg.
Prepare the mixture as above but instead of stuffing a cabbage with it follow the directions below.
Peel and de-vein the whole prawns but leave the tails on. Coat them in in tapioca flour then rinse with the chicken stock.
Wrap and firmly press the mixture around each prawn and place on the cabbage leaf rounds.
Glaze with the egg yolk and steam until cooked.

Pad Pak Boong

Morning Glory with Fermented Soybean

1 tablespoon of fermented soybean
2-3 medium red chillies bruised in a pestle and mortar
3 handfuls of morning glory washed well and cut into long strips
2 tablespoons of vegetable oil
1 tablespoon of chopped garlic
2-3 tablespoons of chicken stock - see page 10 for instructions
1/2 tablespoon of fish sauce
1 tablespoon of light soy sauce

Gently combine the fermented soybeans, chillies and morning glory in a bowl and set aside.
Heat the oil in a pan and fry the garlic until golden brown. then throw in the morning glory mixture.
Add the stock, cover and steam until the morning glory is cooked.
Gradually season with fish sauce and soy sauce tasting as you go as the saltiness of the yellow beans varies a lot.

Place on a serving platter and serve with steamed jasmine rice.

Vegetables

Yam Pak Grob

Spicy Deep Fried Vegetables with Chilli Jam

This is another great use of chilli jam and although I have suggested the vegetables here you can use up any vegetables that you have around.

Tempura Batter Ingredients:
85g of plain flour
1/2 teaspoon of table salt
1/2 teaspoon of sugar
200ml of chilled sparkling water

Other Ingredients:
2 cups of tempura batter
a handful of morning glory washed well and torn into pieces
a handful of young kale leaves washed well and torn into pieces
a handful of string beans washed well and cut into pieces
a handful of long aubergine washed well and cut into pieces
2 cups of coconut cream - see page 8 for instructions
1 cup of chilli jam - see page 66 for recipe
1/2 cup of fish sauce
1-2 tablespoons of lime juice
2 long red chillies diced
a cup of rice vinegar

First make the tempura batter and chilli jam.
Combine the flour, salt and sugar in a mixing bowl.
Gradually mix in the chilled water and whisk but do not over whisk as this will cause the gluten to develop and make the batter heavy.

Prepare all the vegetables and heat the oil.

Dip the vegetables in the batter and deep fry them one by one. If you have chosen any with a strong taste or colour make sure that you fry that one last.

Drain the vegetables and allow them to cool.

Meantime warm the coconut cream on a low heat and combine with the chilli jam.
Season with fish sauce and lime juice. Gently heat to combine but do not let it boil hard.

Remove from the heat and pour into a bowl and serve with the vegetables and the sliced chillies in a bowl of rice vinegar as a side dip.

萬事如意
恭喜發財
35 9973356
85-9973356
1644

Pad Pak Gub Hed

Stir Fried Mushrooms and Bok Choi

2 tablespoons of vegetable oil
1 tablespoon of chopped garlic
2 handfuls of bok choi, washed well, leaves separated
1/2 tablespoon of fish sauce
1/2 tablespoons of light soy sauce
1/2 tablespoon of oyster sauce (optional)
1 handful of sliced mushrooms
1-2 tablespoons of stock or water - see page 10 for instructions

Heat the oil in a pan and fry the garlic until golden brown.

Add the bok choi and season with fish sauce, light soy sauce and oyster sauce if using.

Add the mushrooms and water or stock and cook until the bok choi wilts then remove from the heat.

Serve immediately, ideally in the pan, as this needs to be eaten hot.

Pak Faak Thong

Stir Fried Pumpkin with Sweet Basil

2 tablespoons of finely chopped garlic
6 tablespoons of vegetable oil
3-4 birds eye chillies bruised
2 tablespoons of fish sauce
4 cups of diced pumpkin
1 cup of chicken stock - see page 10 for instructions
1 tablespoon of light soy sauce
a pinch of sugar
2 handfuls of sweet basil - washed, de-veined and torn

Fry the garlic in the oil and when it starts to turn golden add the chillies and season with fish sauce. Add the pumpkin and the stock then cover with a closely fitting lid and allow the dish to steam for a few minutes.
When the pumpkin is cooked through, but still firm, season with soy sauce and sugar.
Briefly stir through the basil and remove from the heat.

Place on a serving platter and serve with steamed jasmine rice.

Pad Nue Poo Prik Lueng

Crab and Bean Stir Fry

3 garlic cloves peeled
3 yellow chillies ends removed
2 tablespoons of vegetable oil
400g of cooked crab meat - white meat only
a handful of string beans cut into 2.5cm pieces
1 tablespoon of chicken stock - see page 10 for instructions
2 tablespoons of fish sauce
1 tablespoon of light soy sauce
a pinch of sugar
2 kaffir lime leaves

Pound the garlic and chillies in a pestle and mortar to make a rough paste.
Fry the paste in the oil and once it turns fragrant add the crab and cook quickly whilst gently turning it being careful not to break up the meat.

After 30 seconds add the beans and moisten with the stock and simmer until cooked.
Season with the fish sauce, soy sauce and a pinch of sugar.
De-vein the lime leaves, tear them and put them in the dish.

Remove from the heat and serve with rice.

Noodles and Stir Frys

Yam Woonsen

Glass Noodle Salad

50g of glass noodles
5 tablespoons of pork minced with a cleaver
12 large raw prawns peeled and de-veined
2 cloves of garlic
a pinch of sea salt
2-4 birds eye or small red chillies
3 tablespoon of sliced shallots
2 tablespoons of fish sauce
2 tablespoons of lime juice
1/2 teaspoon of caster sugar - optional - you don't need this if the pork is sweet
3 tablespoons of dried shrimp deep fried
2 tablespoons of Chinese celery cut into thin strips plus some leaves

Soak the glass noodles in warm water then drain when soft.

Cook the pork in a small amount of boiling water and then remove from the heat and drain retaining the resultant stock.

Cook the prawns in a small amount of boiling water, remove from the heat and drain then stir in with the pork.

Pound the garlic, salt and birds eye chillies together to form a coarse paste and set aside.

Add the paste and half of the shallots to the pork and prawn mixture and stir well.

Add the glass noodles, mix well and season with fish sauce and lime juice balancing and adjusting to taste. Use some of the reserved stock if you need to and also add sugar if you are using it.

Gently stir in the dried shrimp.

Check the seasoning and balance if necessary then finally garnish with the remaining shallots and celery leaves.

This is a great refreshing zingy dish and it's virtually fat free!

Dancers at the floating market

Yam Woonsen for lunch!

Pad Si-Ew

Stir Fried Noodles with Sweet Soy Sauce

Pad Si-Ew has a lot of Chinese influence so I hesitated to include it but I think you will find it such a lovely and handy dish - plus I love it!

4 tablespoons of vegetable oil
2 tablespoons of chopped garlic
300g of sliced pork
2 tablespoons of oyster sauce
3 tablespoons of light soy sauce
2 handfuls of rice noodles - you can use fresh or dried but if you use dried you need to soak them
1 whole egg lightly whisked
3 tablespoons of sweet soy sauce
200g of young kale cut into strips

Dip Ingredients:
2 red chillies
2 yellow chillies
1 cup of rice vinegar
2 teaspoons of caster sugar

Heat the oil and fry the chopped garlic until golden.

Add the pork and fry until it has coloured all over and then add the oyster sauce and light soy sauce.

When the pork is cooked add the noodles and egg and season with the sweet soy sauce.

Let the egg set for a moment before stirring gently ensuring that you do not break up the noodles and egg.

Actually if you have a gas cooker and have high heat it is much better to toss the noodles about as they break up less. Cook until the noodles are nearly cooked then throw in the young kale and stir well till wilted.

Remove from the heat and serve with Prik Nahm Som dip.

Prik Nahm Som - Chillies in Vinegar

This is an everyday dip that is always served with noodles but actually it's just great to spice up almost anything.
Simply slice long red or yellow chillies and cover them with rice wine vinegar.
Put a teaspoon of white sugar on one side for each person to sweeten the dish if they prefer.

Pad Kaproa Gai

Stir Fried Chicken with Holy Basil

This dish works equally well with pork either sliced or minced. Its fast and simple and it really is a great everyday recipe. The Thais often serve it with a deep fried egg (Kai Dao) which is lovely and crispy around the edge but it is still soft and gooey inside. Just drop an egg into hot oil and watch it puff up!

4 tablespoons of vegetable oil
6 garlic cloves chopped or pounded in a pestle and mortar
6-10 birds eye chillies, ends cut off then pounded in a pestle and mortar
500g of boneless chicken breast sliced or minced by hand with a cleaver
2 tablespoons of chicken stock - see page 10 for instructions
1 tablespoon of fish sauce
1 tablespoon of light soy sauce
a handful of holy basil
2 red chillies - shredded (these are for decoration so are optional)
1 egg per person to serve (optional)
vegetable oil to deep fry the egg (optional)

Heat the oil and fry the garlic and chilli until it starts to take on colour.
Add the chicken and when the chicken is cooked add the chicken stock.
Do not overcook this only takes a few minutes.
Season with the fish sauce and soy sauce.
Quickly stir through the holy basil and then remove from the heat.
Sprinkle with the strips of chilli and serve with rice and a deep fried egg and the salty chilli dip.

Prik Nahm Pla - Salty Chilli Dip

This is an everyday dip, simple and quick to put together, simply mix the following.

5 sliced green birds eye chillies
5 sliced medium red chillies
2 cloves of garlic cut into rounds
3 tablespoons of fish sauce
2 tablespoons of lime juice

Use more or less lime according to strength but the flavour of the lime and fish sauce should be equally balanced.

Pad Prik King Tua Faakyow

Stir Fried Pork and Beans

Paste Ingredients:
3 tablespoons of large dried red chillies cut into 5cm pieces soaked until soft then seeds removed
a pinch of sea salt
1 1/2 tablespoons of sliced galangal
3 tablespoons of sliced lemongrass
1 teaspoon of coriander root scraped
2 teaspoons of kaffir lime leaves
1 tablespoon of garlic
2 tablespoons of shallots
1 tablespoon of dry roasted shrimp paste

Other Ingredients:
200g of pork belly diced
2 tablespoons of vegetable oil
3 tablespoons of red curry paste
1 tablespoon of fish sauce
1 tablespoon of light soy sauce
1 tablespoon of palm sugar
250g of string beans washed and cut into 2.5cm pieces
1 tablespoon of chicken stock - see page 10 for instructions
3-4 finely shredded lime leaves

First make the red curry paste - see page 12 for instructions.

Fry the pork belly without putting any oil in the pan to render its fat.
If you don't get enough oil from this and it starts to stick to the pan then add in a little oil as it cooks.
When the pork has browned set it aside.

Fry the paste in the oil until it starts to smell fragrant then add in the pork and fry until it is cooked.

Season with the fish sauce, light soy sauce and palm sugar.

Add in the string beans and stock and continue stirring until the beans are cooked but still have some bite.

Remove from the heat and serve sprinkled with the shredded lime leaves.

Finely shred lime leaves by removing the central stalks, put a few half leaves together and roll them like a cigar then finely slice from the end.

Nem Phat Wunsen

Cured Pork with Pickled Garlic

This is a great quick lunch and it's delicious served with rice and Gang Jude - see page 55

2 tablespoons of vegetable oil
2 tablespoons of chopped garlic
25g of glass noodles pre-soaked to soften them if they are dried
1 tablespoon of fish sauce
200g of cured pork - this can be bought at oriental shops for a speedy lunch
1 egg lightly beaten
10 whole pickled garlic outer sheaths removed and cloves separated and chopped if large
1 teaspoon of sugar (optional)
1/2 cup of spring onions cut into 5cm stalks

Break up the cured pork with your hands until it crumbles then set it aside.

Heat the oil and fry the garlic until it is crispy.

Add the pork and fish sauce to the garlic then cook until golden.

When the pork is cooked stir in the noodles and cook for another two minutes.

Add in the lightly beaten egg and allow it to set a bit before you gently fold it in until it is cooked.
In this way you get some bigger pieces in the final dish which makes it more like broken omelette than scrambled egg.

Stir in the pickled garlic.

If it is not sweet enough add the sugar and adjust the fish sauce if necessary.

At this stage add all the flavourings gradually and taste as you go because the saltiness of the pork will vary.

Lower the heat and gently stir in the spring onions.

Put onto a serving plate and serve immediately.

Khao Soi

Chiang Mai Noodles

Everyone loves this dish because your guests decide the level of seasoning themselves as they eat it and as an added bonus it keeps well - indeed it is one of those rare Thai dishes that improve in the fridge overnight.

Paste Ingredients:
2 tablespoons of dried long red chillies soaked and de-seeded
1 1/2 tablespoons of sliced shallots
1 tablespoon of sliced garlic
2 coriander roots - scraped
1 tablespoon of Gaeng Hang Lae curry powder - see page 16 for recipe
1/2 teaspoon of root ginger

Other Ingredients:
500ml of coconut cream see - see page 8 for instructions
250ml of water
1 cup of chicken stock - see page 10 for instructions
600g of chicken thighs - these must be on the bone with the skin removed
4 pandanus leaves cut into 5cm strips
8 cubes of ginger cut into 1cm cubes
a pinch of table salt
1 teaspoon of palm sugar
2 teaspoons of fish sauce
300g of fresh egg noodles
1 tablespoon of coarsely chopped coriander leaves
1 spring onion coarsely chopped
3-4 deep fried large chillies to use as decoration
2 limes cut into 8 pieces

Pickled Mustard Green Condiment Ingredients:
250g of pickled mustard greens
1 tablespoons of caster sugar
8 shallots peeled and sliced
juice of 1 lime

Chilli Garlic Dip - Prik Bon Pat
Fry 3-4 tablespoons of chilli powder in a cup of coconut milk over a low heat for a few minutes. You will see the oil rise to the top and this indicates that it is ready - allow to cool before serving.

Pickled Mustard Green Condiment - Pak Dong
Drain the pickled mustard greens and wash several times very thoroughly.
Pick off all the dark green leaves and discard the stems.
Stir 1 tablespoon of caster sugar into a bowl of water and soak the mustard greens in it.
Peel and slice 8 shallots and soak them in water with the juice of a lime.
Leave these both for thirty minutes then drain and mix together.
Put on one side until ready to serve but do not refrigerate as this arrests the development.

Now to work.........

Before you get going you need to make the following preparations. You can do these a day in advance if you like.

1. First make the paste.

2. Deep fry a handful of the noodles in hot oil until they puff up, reserving the rest of them for later. Drain the noodles then put to one side to use as topping.

3. Make up the pickled mustard green condiment.

4. Make up the chilli garlic dip.

Serves Four

Now for the Curry!

Remove all the chicken fat and skin from the chicken thighs.

Put half of the coconut cream and 250ml of water and half a cup of stock in a pan and add the chicken thighs.
Add the pandanus leaves, ginger cubes and a pinch of salt.
Bring to the boil and simmer until tender.

In a separate pan add 10 tablespoons of coconut cream, bring to the boil for a minute then add the paste and cook until the oil just starts to begin to separate stirring all the time. Gradually add some of the sauce from the chicken pot to keep it moist. During this process add a pinch of table salt.
You should maintain a creamy consistency.

Remove the chicken from the poaching stock and gently put it into the paste sauce and stir slowly.

Add the remaining coconut cream, chicken stock and a pinch of salt to the poaching liquid and keep simmering.
You are now going to be using this poaching stock to moisten the chicken but you only want to use about half of it as later we need the other half.

Add a teaspoon of palm sugar and the fish sauce to the chicken and gradually use the poaching stock to moisten this dish slowly adding one ladle at a time and incorporating well before adding the next. Be patient!

Boil the noodles in salted water for a few minutes until cooked then drain in cold water.

Put the cooked noodles in the bottom of 4 serving bowls and top with a ladle of the poaching stock liquid.
Put a piece of chicken in a bowl and ladle the sauce on top of that.

Top each bowl with crispy noodles and sprinkle with coriander leaves, chopped spring onion and whole deep fried chillies to serve.

Please note that the final chicken sauce on its own can taste a little salty but once it is all put together the flavour balances out and is correct.

Serve with:

The chilli garlic dip
The pickled mustard green condiment
Raw fresh cut beans
Raw savoy or Chinese cabbage sliced
A small bowl of fish sauce
A small bowl of sugar
The cut limes

Gobgaew presenting her dessert for Thai Airlines 1994

Gobgaew studying home economics top row 2nd from the right

Desserts

Kanom Tua Pap

Moong Bean Pancakes

1/2 cup of sesame seeds dry fried until they smell great
2 tablespoons of caster sugar
1 cup of split moong beans
a pandanus leaf
3 tablespoons of water
2 cups of sticky rice flour
warm water
a few drops of Hales Blue Boy red syrup
2 cups of grated young coconut and some for garnish
a teaspoon of table salt

Mix 3/4 of the sesame seeds with the sugar and set aside. Keep the additional 1/4 to use later.
Boil the moong beans until cooked and set aside.
Pound the pandanus leaf with the water and then squeeze and remove the leaf by hand to extract the coloured water.
Mix the flour with enough warm water to make a dough and knead well for a long time until it becomes very pliable.
Separate the mixture into three equal batches and colour one with the pandanus colour, one with the red colour and leave one white.
Mix the moong beans with the chopped coconut (reserving some coconut as topping) and add the salt.
Roll the flour mixture into balls and flatten until thin then boil in water until they float to the top then remove and allow to become cool enough to handle.
Stuff these pancakes with the moong bean mixture and fold over.

Serve topped with the remaining young coconut and sesame seeds.

This dish really takes some practice but it's great fun to try!

Khao Neow Peeg Lam Yai

Sticky Rice with Logan and Coconut Milk

This dish benefits from washing the rice through with alum rock which gives it a translucent finish X

2 cups of sticky rice -soaked overnight
a piece of alum rock - see page 17
2 knotted pandanus leaves
1 1/2 cups of caster sugar
2 cups of peeled logan fruit
1 1/2 cups of thick coconut milk or even cream - see page 8 for instructions
1/2 teaspoon of table salt

Soak the rice overnight then rinse well and wash thoroughly combing through with the alum rock if you are using it. If you do you will visibly see that each grain turns shiny.
Cook the rice by steaming it with the knotted pandanus leaves on top until it is cooked.
Alternatively you can cook in a rice cooker according to manufacturers instructions.
Remove from heat and immediately stir in the sugar and logan.
Stir well until all the sugar dissolves.
Warm the coconut milk on a low heat and season with salt.
Serve the rice in a bowls and ladle the coconut milk on top.

Note: You can use any similar fresh fruit like lychee or even tinned lychee.

Ning's Tip X

This is nice topped with a few steamed kidney beans as it gives the dish an added crunch. As you have to pre-soak dried beans overnight and boil them it is better to use tinned kidney beans which are ready to eat. Wash them well before you cook them though because the liquid they are stored in is pretty gloopy.

Alum Rock

Tap Tim Grob

Water Chestnuts in Syrup and Coconut Milk

I love to see these in little bags in the markets. When I first saw them I thought that they were pomegranate seeds and it never ceases to amaze new guests at dinner parties when I tell them they are water chestnuts. It is really important that you use freshly made coconut milk for this as tinned milk will just taste too artificial.

140g of canned water chestnuts
1/4 cup of Hales Blue Boy red syrup or pomegranate juice
1 cup of water
1 cup of caster sugar
1/4 cup of tapioca flour - you can use cornflour if you can't source this
crushed ice for serving
1/2 cup of thick coconut milk - do not use canned, make fresh for this dish - see page 8 for instructions
a pinch of table salt
a pinch of sugar
1/2 cup of coconut cream - see page 8 for instructions

Drain the water chestnuts then cut them into into very small pomegranate seed sized pieces. Soak them in the Blue Boy red syrup or pomegranate juice for thirty minutes.

In the meantime, put the water and sugar in a pan and heat until the sugar dissolves and simmer until it becomes a thick syrup then put to one side.

Sieve the flour. Drain the chestnuts, spread the flour on a tray and roll them in it.

Shake off the excess flour and boil the chestnuts in the syrup until they rise to the top then blanch in cold water and drain.

Divide the crushed ice between two serving bowls, top with chestnuts and finally the coconut milk.

Serve with some thick coconut cream with a small amount of salt and sugar added.

A Sweet Little Tip for You X

If you need to thicken coconut milk boil it whilst stirring constantly .

Kanom Gluay

Banana Puddings

*You will need some small ceramic cups to make these.
You could use Chinese teacups which should measure about 1.5" or you can take the traditional route and make little cups yourself out of banana leaves.*

2 cups of small mashed banana - they must be soft but not brown
1/2 tablespoon of rice flour
4 tablespoons of tapioca flour
2 tablespoons of arrowroot flour
1/2 to 3/4 cup of palm sugar with a pinch of salt added
1/3 of a cup of coconut cream (I find that tinned works well in this recipe because often the coconuts we get in the UK do not make it possible to make the cream thick enough) or see page 8 for instructions
shredded coconut to decorate

Mash the bananas and sieve them through a fine sieve.
Mix the flours, sugar and coconut cream with the bananas. If the palm sugar is too hard soften it by heating it in the microwave with a few drops of water.
Steam the cups before adding the mixture in the pots to prevent the mixture becoming soggy.
Place the mixture in the small ceramic cups and steam for thirty minutes.
Decorate with grated coconut and serve immediately.

Banana Puddings

Coconut Agar Agar Sweets

Wun Gati

Coconut Agar Agar Sweets

These soft and lovely desserts are surprisingly easy to make but you have to make real coconut milk as tinned milk makes these like bullets.
The agar agar stiffens up with age so it's best to eat them within 12 hours of making.

Green Layer Ingredients:
5 pandanus leaves cut into 5cm pieces
1 cup of water
1 teaspoon of agar agar
1/2 cup of caster sugar
1 cup of young coconut milk, or water if you can't get this
some pieces of small chopped young coconut if using the young coconut milk

White Layer Ingredients:
1 cup of water
1 teaspoon of agar agar
1/2 cup of caster sugar
1 teaspoon of table salt
1 cup of coconut cream - see page 8 for instructions

Make up the two types of coconut milk and set aside.

To make the white layer:
Put the water in the pan and bring to the boil then sprinkle with the agar agar and stir until dissolved.
Add the sugar and salt and stir until dissolved then add in the coconut cream and reheat.

Pour the liquid to the halfway point in either moulds or small glasses and refrigerate until set then go on to make the second layer as follows.

To make the green layer:
Pound the pandanus leaves with a couple of tablespoons of water in a pestle and mortar to extract the colour then strain and add the coloured liquid to the cup of water to make pandanus water.
Put the mixture in the pan and bring to the boil then sprinkle with the agar agar and stir until dissolved.
Add the sugar and stir until dissolved then add in the young coconut milk or water and reheat.
If you are adding in any chopped young coconut then do it now.

Top up the desserts and refrigerate to set as this speeds up the process and gives a nicer finish.

Kanom Mew Gaeng

Baked Moong Bean and Coconut Custard

This is a two part recipe first make the dessert as it is shown in the top image or even serve it in a big dish topped with deep fried shallots. or continue onto the second stage shown below.

2 cups of yellow split moong beans
1/2 cup of real coconut cream - see page 8 or canned milk or cream would be ok to use for this as it is often quite difficult to get coconuts in the UK that will make the milk thick enough
3/4 cup of palm sugar

Put the split moong beans in a pan and add enough water to cover and boil until the beans are soft and cooked. Drain,mash and set aside.
Heat the coconut cream and sugar in a small pan and add the beans with a pinch of salt and cook until the mixture is stiff.
Place the mixture into small moulds, refrigerate and serve when set or use it to make mock jackfruit balls.

If you are feeling ambitious you can use the mixture to make the more sophisticated and skilled mock jackfruit balls.

Met Kanom - Mock Jackfruit Balls

3 cups of Jasmine water - see page 18 for Tienne Op candle instructions
1 cup of caster sugar
a pinch of table salt
10 egg yolks lightly whisked

Roll the mixture into oval balls - baked bean shaped ideally but three times the size.
Make a syrup out of the jasmine water, sugar and salt and simmer until thickened.
During this process you will need to occasionally add some extra water to replace the water that evaporates. Try and keep the water at the same level throughout.
Dip the balls, one by one, into egg yolk and cook in the syrup.
You will know when they are ready when the egg starts to turn a darker yellow and the texture changes.
Remove and allow to cool before eating.

Mock jackfruit balls are a delightful challenge to make!

Khaew Niaw Mamuang

Sticky Rice with Mango

Recipe serves four to six

Mae taught me a great trick to make the rice shine. When you wash the rice you wash it through with some Alum rock because it gives a translucent quality to the rice..

250g of sticky rice - soaked overnight
a piece of alum rock - see page 17
2 pandanus leaves - washed well and knotted
1 cup of coconut milk - see page 8 for instructions
2/3rd cup of caster sugar
1 teaspoon of table salt
2 large mangoes peeled and sliced
3/4 cup of coconut cream - see page 8 for instructions
a sprinkle of dried split moong beans for topping (optional)

Soak the rice overnight then rinse well and wash thoroughly combing through with the alum rock if you are using it.
If you do you will visibly see that each grain turns shiny.
Cook the rice by steaming it with the knotted pandanus leaves on top until it is cooked.
Alternatively you can cook it in a rice cooker according to manufacturers instructions.

Heat the coconut milk until warm in a small pan and add the sugar and salt, stir well until all the sugar has dissolved. It is crucial to stir continuously otherwise the oil will separate.
Remove from the heat and add in the rice when it is cooked and stir really well.

Cover and leave to stand for at least fifteen minutes in a warm place before serving.

Taste and adjust if necessary - you should have a sweet taste with a balance of saltiness.

Peel and slice the mango and serve with a topping of coconut cream with a pinch of salt stirred in.

To make the topping: in the photo (optional)
Wash a cup of yellow peeled mung beans and soak them for an hour in warm water.
Dry thoroughly and then slowly dry fry over a very low heat until they pop open a little..
Allow to cool and then store in an airtight jar for future use.

Gati Tangthai Karnoon

Melon and Jackfruit in Jasmine Infused Coconut Milk

1/2 cup of coconut cream - see page 8 for instructions
Tienne Op Candle or jasmine flavouring - see page 18 for details
a handful of edible jasmine flowers - optional
1 cup of melon balls
1/2 cup of jackfruit
1/2 cup of palm sugar
1 teaspoon of table salt
2 cups of crushed ice

First make up the coconut cream - you really can't use tinned for this recipe. See page 8 for instructions.
To create the perfumed flavour put the coconut cream in a bowl within a large cake tin.
I use a tin so that the candle does not burn the container. Scatter with jasmine flowers if using.
Light the candle at both ends and allow it to burn for a few minutes.
Blow the candle out and quickly put it into the bottom of the tin next to the coconut cream and put the lid on then place in the fridge overnight. The smoke will gently infuse into the liquid giving it a soft sandalwood like scent.

Prepare the fruit and when ready to serve put the crushed ice into individual serving bowls and place the fruit on top.

Remove the jasmine flowers from the cream, stir in the sugar and salt and pour over the fruit.

Please note as the palm sugar we get in the UK is not as pliable as in Thailand it will not integrate into the coconut milk as easily. Therefore you must soften it in the microwave with a touch of water before using.

This delicately smoked recipe uses a traditional Tienne Op candle. These candles are increasingly difficult to find but when you get one it will keep for a long time stored in a box in the fridge.

Index

Index

Items highlighted in pink contain coriander root

Index

Items highlighted in pink contain coriander root

R
rice
grilled pork with sticky rice 112
northern larb with sticky rice 82
pork and rice soup 56
sour Esarn sausage 154
sticky rice with logan and coconut milk 183
sticky rice with mango 191
rice pancakes
steamed pork in rice pancakes 138

Cheers chaps!

As an amateur writing this book I had a big learning curve and needed a little help from my friends......

Luckily I have some very clever friends and I would like to thank them. First and foremost Ning naturally for all her patient help communicating between myself and Mae and always being willing to help despite the distance between us and her very busy life.

My husband Paul for supporting me with the project which has been a labour of love for many years.

Michelle for coming up with all the artwork and inspiring me creatively, I could not have done this without her!

Jonny for fixing my dubious photos and Kat for tasting everything that moves with me !

Also to all my friends especially Lindsey for putting up with whatever was thrown at her whilst the seemingly endless project emerged and to Martin for his proofreading. Also to all my Bangkok friends who have taken me everywhere and eaten half of the country with me, not least of which Atom at the wonderful Chakrabongse villas where I stayed whilst studying Thai at Chulalongkorn University and Chart, Margie and Ross at Eastbank Residence where I stayed many times with an endless stream of friends who visited during my long cooking stretches.

It's been a blast...

Carole X

Me and my beloved Thai pans - reunited!

Photo: Kat Hughes 2017

VIEUX - BOIS
ECOLE HOTELIERE
DE GENEVE